Indoor Plants
A Popular Guide

Indoor Plants
A Popular Guide

Brian & Valerie Proudley

BLANDFORD PRESS
Poole   Dorset

First published in the U.K. in 1981 by Blandford Press,
Link House, West Street, Poole, Dorset, BH15 1LL

Copyright © 1981 Blandford Books Ltd.
Reprinted 1981
Distributed in the United States by
Sterling Publishing Co., Inc.,
2 Park Avenue, New York, N.Y. 10016

British Library Cataloguing in Publication Data

Proudley, Brian
  Indoor plants in colour.
  1. House plants
  I. Title II. Proudley, Valerie
  635.9′65   SB419

ISBN 0 7137 1003 9

Typeset by Tonbridge Printers Ltd., Tonbridge, Kent
Printed in Hong Kong by South China Printing Company

Contents

Acknowledgements

We wish to thank the following companies/organisations/individuals for their kind cooperation in providing access to their plants for photographic purposes. All are located in the Auckland area of New Zealand.
Palmers Nurseries; Orinda Nursery (Howick); Zealandia Nurseries
The Seventh-Day Adventist Hospital (St. Heliers)
Mrs Rosalei Peach; Mr Frank Goudie
Steve and Bob of the Domain Nursery, Auckland City Council
Chris of Sunhill Garden Centre (St. John's)

Introduction

There can be little doubt that modern interiors, with their emphasis on natural materials and surfaces, are enhanced by the careful use of bold glossy-leaved specimen plants. These have the ability to soften hard lines or break up expanses of monotone. Colourful 'accent' plants can add considerable interest to otherwise stark decor. Present-day private homes are light and warm, often having double-glazed windows with walls and ceiling spaces insulated against extremes of temperature. These conditions favour the growth of indoor plants. When they grow well and flourish, the cultivator is encouraged to try his hand at growing others. As sales increase, the nurseryman continually seeks new lines to add to the existing range and thus it goes on, demand creating supplies of fresh material. Fortunately there is a great variety to draw on. From the purely practical point of view, weighing the cost against that of permanent plants and temporary cut flowers must be a good reason for so many people choosing to decorate their homes with living plants.

What are indoor plants?

No plants can be classed as natural indoor plants. Nurserymen and florists have had to search out those kinds which grow under low light intensity and which are able to tolerate a greater fluctuation of temperature, as well as generally drier air, than they would enjoy in their native habitats. Several indoor plant species come from tropical or sub-tropical forest areas of the globe. Others, such as the popular cacti and succulents, grow naturally in more arid places. The term 'indoor plants' covers a wide variety of plant types of which a collection may include trees, shrubs, climbers, herbaceous species, bulbs, tubers or even annuals. Although some plants may be placed outside for part of the year, in this book we shall concentrate on those species suited to more or less permanent indoor culture. Further interest can be provided by using temporary indoor flowering pot plants.

Plants in the home

All plants, excluding most fungi and a few orchids, will soon die if denied sufficient light to meet their natural day-length requirement. In order to fulfil their vital functions correctly, plants need both atmospheric and soil moisture as well as a periodic change of air. Most plants grow better in a fluctuating day/night temperature where at night-time the air is a few degrees cooler than during the day. When grown in pots, as most indoor plants are, extra feeding, in addition to the fertiliser content of the compost they are in, is also desirable. When growing naturally, plants flourish only where conditions suit them best. Should the weather become dry they can send down roots in search of moisture; if conditions are shady they bend their leaves to catch every glimmer of life-giving sunlight. When growing any plants in pots, in an often hostile environment, you have to provide extra care, for your charges are unable to fend for themselves. Obviously then, plants grow best indoors in positions which nearly duplicate their natural environment. The different rooms in your home should provide various degrees of light, shade and warmth. Bearing these points in mind, try to select your plants carefully to suit the location, remembering that an harmonious balance between light, moisture, air, temperature and feeding is essential.

Light

If their full individual potential is to be realised, indoor plants must be well-positioned to ensure that they receive their daily light requirement, light being the regulating factor in all plant growth. Compared with a plant growing in the garden, a similar individual placed behind a window receives less than half the amount of light and mid-way into a normally sun-lit room the proportion is less than a quarter. Fortunately, many of the species which we cultivate indoors are naturally shade-lovers and so are perfectly able to cope with low light conditions. The dark leathery-leaved sorts of house plants are, generally, the best equipped to thrive in these places. Those with leaf variegation require rather more light — but not direct sun, if they are to retain this feature. Purple-leaved plants normally come into this group too. Most flowering sorts (including temporary pot plants) need the brightest positions. Plants such as cacti and succulents, which require dry soil for much of the year, also favour light positions and will tolerate direct sun although most of them dislike being baked alive in their pots.

Water

This is the second factor vital to plant growth; indeed plants, like most animals, are largely composed of water. Also, without moisture, chemicals remain locked in the soil and are unavailable for the plant's use. Problems associated with watering are unfortunately the single biggest headache for the novice indoor 'gardener'. Generally too much water at the wrong time rather than too little causes the failures. In the cultivation of plants indoors, it is of prime importance to regulate the watering according to individual need. Those species which develop a weak root system, for example, will require less water than a fibrous-rooted plant in a similar-sized pot.

As mentioned previously, light and temperature, as well as water, must be in direct proportion to one another. During the low light/temperature conditions of winter, many plants become (or attempt to become) semi-dormant. At this time, watering has to be adjusted accordingly. It is far better to err on the dry side than the wet; it is easier to revive a wilting plant with a good soak than salvage something of a plant with a decayed root system! Increased amounts of water may be given when temperatures are higher and light will stimulate growth.

Although some plants naturally require more water than others, very few species can tolerate permanently wet compost for very long. The age of the specimen, the size of its container, type of compost — and, most importantly, the temperature of the room, together with its atmosphere, all have a bearing on the frequency of watering. Pots should be checked by feeling the compost with the fingers or, better still, by weighing the pot in the hand. If similar composts are used, you will very soon become proficient in determining the difference in weight between a dry and a waterlogged one. No pots should be allowed to dry to the extent that the compost actually shrinks away from the sides of the pot.

Plant roots require air as well as water. When cold and saturated, all the soil air spaces are filled with water so the action of most beneficial bacteria ceases and harmful fungus diseases proliferate, causing the death of root ends, which, more often than not, means the demise of the plant. Experience will also enable you to group your plants mentally according to their needs. Very few can remain wet — these are naturally lovers of bog conditions. With many, you may be liberal during their active growing season then, at other times, you must keep the compost just moist. Other plants prefer the compost to be partially dry between waterings so that their roots really have to search for moisture and these are the most susceptible to over-watering during dull weather.

Most pots may be watered with a narrow spout can from above, filling the space between the compost and the pot rim as many times as is needed to allow excess to run from the drainage holes in the base. Always allow the compost to drain through completely before replacing the pots in their saucers or covers. Surplus water which gathers in the saucer must be tipped away. Bowls seldom have drainage holes and here special care is needed to ensure that surplus water is not allowed to stagnate.

Some plants, particularly those with hairy leaves, object to being watered over their leaves. Saintpaulias are particularly difficult to water in the conventional way. With these, place the pots up to their middles in a bowl of water instead. Never use icy-cold water direct from the tap for tropical indoor plants as this lowers the soil temperature and is likely to cause a shock to the plant's root system. Ideally, the water should be drawn several hours previously, enabling the temperature to rise naturally. It is, of course, also possible to warm the water by adding a little hot water to it. Normal tap water additives, such as chlorine and fluoride, can harm certain plants, turning their leaves blotchy and their tips brown. The gas in chlorinated water will disperse if the water is first run into a wide-mouthed container an hour or so before use. When fluoride is the cause of noticeable damage you may have to resort to giving your plants rain or pond water instead. Softened water can also be harmful to sensitive plants. Where water is 'hard', a white deposit may be left on leaves.

Atmosphere

Walk through a forest or into a glass-house on a warm day and you will quickly detect the humid atmosphere which living plants enjoy. This humidity is lacking in our homes, the air being too dry for the comfort of many plants. Their well-being is assured if the moisture content in the air surrounding them is increased. One way of achieving this in warm weather is to mist over the plants using a hand-held atomiser filled with clean water. A moist micro-climate can also be provided if the pots are plunged into a planter containing moist peat. Instead of peat, some people prefer to stand the pots on a layer of pebbles which receives periodic tricklings of water. Like us, plants require freely circulating air for they too have to breathe. Under normal indoor conditions there is sufficient movement of air caused, for example, by the opening and closing of doors.

On fine days during the autumn, every advantage should be taken to see that your plants have as much air and light as possible. This guarantees sturdy growth with ripened stems — essential for cooler days ahead. Although plants appreciate fresh air, very few indeed can tolerate cold draughts for very long. Where plants are placed on inside window-sills, do check for draughts first. Some subjects, such as maidenhair fern, are damaged irreparably when placed in a cold airstream. Fumes from fires — either coal, gas or oil, can also be damaging to sensitive species. The slightest leak overnight will hinder development.

Temperature

Elsewhere in this book we may have appeared to suggest that growing plants indoors is a relatively new phenomenon. This was not intended for we well know of the splendid pot plants which grandmother (or great-grandmother) tended so lovingly on her cottage window-sill. Grown in such situations, they tolerated the conditions well, for lace curtains shaded them from the hot sun, then, when nights turned colder, heavier material protected them from frost. Today's houses, with their large windows, are light, mostly well heated in winter or, in hot countries, air-conditioned in summer. At first these would appear to be the ideal conditions for plants but unfortunately this is not always so. Central heating systems warm rooms during the evening and night, the very time when most plants prefer to be cooler. Modern heating means a dry atmosphere instead of the moist or humid air which the majority of plants enjoy. In spite of these seeming obstacles, the wide range of plant material available today ensures that our rooms can be decorated with luxuriant, living greenery.

The ideal average temperature for indoor plants is in the range of 15–21°C (59–70°F) during the day and 7–10°C (44.5–50°F) at night. Most plants, provided that they are healthy, well ripened and have an established root system, are able to tolerate lower temperatures for short periods during the resting period of their growth cycle. Few tropical plants, when in active growth, can survive temperatures much lower than 5°C (41°F) without damage. It is surprising just how many plants we grow indoors today which, in years gone by, were kept in warm glass-houses and brought into the house on special occasions.

Plant names

Latin plant names are often a source of concern to novice gardeners. They are nonetheless of prime importance to those who take their horticulture seriously. Such people reason that, because these names are precise, little room is left for doubt as to the true identity of a plant — a fault which is frequent when 'common' names only are used. However, for the home gardener, who is unlikely to correspond (especially internationally)about his or her plants, the use of everyday common names may prove easier. Most of these have been cherished for many years, often reflecting something of the plants' personalities.

The big drawback with common names is that the same name can on occasion be applied to more than one plant! Also a single plant may over the years have accumulated several names. Add to this the common names of the plant in the vernacular of the country where it is being grown and the list gets longer all the time! For this reason the professional grower prefers to use a plant's botanical name. These names are composed of at least two, sometimes three, Latinised words. (We say 'Latinised', for they are, in fact, mostly derived from other languages.)

The first word is the generic, or group, name which is shared by other closely related species, e.g. *Aglaonema*. The second word, the specific name, belongs to only one species within that group, e.g. *Aglaonema commutatum*. Sometimes there is a third word to complete the name, e.g. *Aglaonema commutatum* var. *maculatum*. This happens when a species — the basis of biological classification — produces fixed natural variants in the wild. These *vars*, as they are known (from the Latin *varietas*), retain their individual characteristics when brought into cultivation. In addition, there are cultivars. This is a group of man-maintained variants of special importance to gardeners for among them are some of the finest plants we grow. Garden-raised, they can be recognised in books and catalogues by the way in which their 'fancy names' are printed in Roman type and are contained within single quotation marks, e.g. *Aglaonema* 'Silver Queen'.

The rather loose term 'hybrid' is used to describe plants resulting from crosses between two individuals. Their names are styled according to the nature of the cross, as follows: (a) individuals of the same species, as for cultivar, (b) two individuals of different species of the same genus, e.g. *Caladium* × *hortulanum*, (c) species of different genera, e.g. × *Fatshedera lizei*. These three types of hybrid can be met with in house plants. When the parentage of garden hybrids is unknown, specific names are not printed. Neither is the × (hybrid) sign used for plant crosses between two individuals of the same species.

We mentioned that Latin plant names are favoured by the plantsman because they are precise. They also indicate the relationship between plants and, because of this, there is constant research into plant names, resulting in all too frequent changes when one name supplants another. The reasons for this are several. The systematic taxonomist, as the botanist is called whose special concern these researches are, may decide that several species, although obviously very closely related, are too dissimilar to be included under the one generic 'umbrella'. This happened sometime ago to the genus *Aralia*, a favourite for indoors, which is now split into *Dizygotheca*, *Fatsia*, *Schefflera* etc. Gardeners often prefer to continue using the original name which, once it has been superseded, is termed a synonym (syn.).

Choice of plants

Here we come to the main object of the book for, provided that you do not regard indoor plants as simply part of your furnishings, you will, by careful consideration of the conditions existing in your home and wise selection, be certain to choose a suitable species. This is better than obtaining your plant first then trying to find a place for it. Indoor plants come in a wide variety of shapes and sizes to suit all requirements. There are erect growing kinds, such as *Ficus*, *Philodendron* and *Sansevieria*, some of which eventually need plenty of head-room. Climbers require the support of trellis, bamboo poles or cords suspended from the ceiling. Trailers, e.g. *Tradescantia* and *Columnea*, need to be placed high up, perhaps on a shelf or in a hanger, for their drooping stems to be displayed to advantage. Mixed bowls, in which a selection of plants are accommodated, should be planted so that leaf or flower colours are complementary, with growth rate balanced.

Smaller bowls are most effective when placed upon a low table. Living screens of greenery, either light or dense, can be arranged according to needs. We have seen ivy, *Hedera*, trained up several cords behind a sunless window, effectively blocking out the unsightly rear of a neighbouring town house. In open plan interiors, room dividers are softened by the careful placing of indoor plants. In these situations, bold-growing specimens can, by breaking the line of vision, themselves become effectual room dividers. As we have mentioned elsewhere, the dark glossy-leaved sorts can tolerate positions offering the least amount of available light. Consequently they are frequently placed in corners where they recede naturally into the background. Brightly coloured or architectur-ally interesting kinds have to be positioned with caution for, if too many 'accent plants' are used, they will clamour for visual attention. There is little doubt, however, that, when used with discretion, these magnificent individuals become an important part of a room layout. In a small room, as in a small garden, the temptation is to scale down the size of the plants accordingly. This is a mistake. A better balance is obtained by the bold inclusion of one or two large specimens rather than several small pots. Also, in small rooms, an illusion of space can be created immediately by the use of a mirrored wall to reflect the plants.

Acclimatisation

Indoor plants may be purchased at any time of the year and, if the weather is inclement, your caring for the plant must start as soon as it is in your hands. To minimise shock from a

11

sudden change in temperature, first ensure that it is protected on its journey from the garden centre or florist. Next, because the atmosphere in greenhouses is invariably more humid than in a normal living room situation, the tendency is for plants to have produced fewer roots than required for their new position. Much can be done to help a plant at this time by placing it in a cooler position indoors, with some shade, rather than putting it in the place for which it is ultimately destined. A twice daily misting over (depending on other conditions) will be a great help to the plant in the acclimatisation period.

Feeding

Strange as it may seem, many beginners appear to care for their new charges well by siting them carefully and systematically watering them, but then totally neglect the fact that, after the plants have exhausted the feeding element in the compost, frequent feeding will be required. This is another factor which is linked to prevailing conditions. For example, you do not feed a plant which is dormant or has been recently re-potted. Nor do already sickly-looking individuals take kindly to stimulants offered. The modern resin-coated or time-release granules containing a balanced fertiliser are of particular value to the grower of house plants. These may be incorporated in the compost then, when exhausted (you can determine this either by the time-life of the product or by the empty cases on the compost surface), simply scatter a few more in the pot. Concentrated liquid feeds are also available to the amateur. These should be diluted with a carefully measured amount of tepid water to provide a weak dose at 10-day or 2-week intervals during the active growing season.

There are also foliar feeds which are very efficient when misted over and under the leaves. Foliar feeds are quick-acting on healthy plants. They may also be used successfully on poor plants whose intake of normal water has been reduced for a while. When applying any kind of fertiliser, make certain that the compost is already moist. Bear in mind that there is a real danger of scorching tender roots when dry fertiliser is added to dry compost and then watered in. Always resist the temptation when feeding plants to hurry growth along by applying stronger solutions or more frequent applications than recommended.

Cleaning leaves

Leaves are the main centre of photosynthesis in a plant. Photosynthesis is a process whereby, under the influence of light, the chlorophyll contained in the leaves converts water and carbon dioxide gas, present in the atmosphere, into carbohydrates and oxygen. Although the primary intake of water is through the roots, considerable amounts of water vapour are also both absorbed and exhaled, together with the gases mentioned, through the stomata, or pores, of the underleaf. Because of the importance of this function, quite apart from the appearance of the plant, regular weekly sponging to remove clogging dust is essential. Both upper as well as lower leaf surfaces of smooth–leaved kinds can be washed with water to which a few drops of a proprietary leaf-shine liquid have been added. Some people prefer to use a 50/50 mixture of milk and water instead. Resist the temptation to wipe the leaves with olive oil for, although they gleam at first, this can have a detrimental effect on them. Most hairy-leaved plants dislike water on their leaves. Use a soft brush to gently clean them instead.

Potting and re-potting

Regardless of the method used to propagate them, when your young plants are well rooted is the time to pot them up. Naturally enough, the initial pot size depends on the size or vigour of your subject. Under- rather than over-potting (selecting too large a pot) is best for there is a real danger of surplus compost turning sour before it is utilised by the plant roots, something which invariably happens when the pot is too large. If your pots have been used previously, make certain that they are washed scrupulously clean then sun-dried.

When plants are young, re-potting is frequently required annually for, after a full season's growth, the plants' roots will have used up all the space in their container. When an established plant makes more than usual demands for water this is also an almost certain sign that little free compost is left in the pot and that re-potting is needed. Confirmation of this can be obtained if a mass of roots is seen when the plant is tapped out of its pot. Additionally, some poor plants that have not established well for some reason or other are frequently improved by potting back. This is the opposite to potting on and, instead of using a larger pot for the move, the compost is reduced and a smaller pot used. It must be understood that not all plants require frequent re-potting, even when their pots are filled with roots. Most of the splendid, long-lived Palm family fall into this category. These continue for many seasons in a comparatively small container. After potting or re-potting, always water the plants gently but thoroughly, placing them in the shade for a day or so. Allow the compost to become dry between each of the first few waterings because some plants become a little lazy at making fresh roots when they are receiving liberal amounts of water without having to search for it.

Top-dressing

An annual top-dressing with fresh compost is normally sufficient for established plants in large pots. Before carrying out the top-dressing remove about 5 cm (1 in) or more of old soil and roots from the top of the pot. Whenever possible, all potting operations carried out at home should be done in the early spring when the roots are most active.

Pruning and shaping

Except when it interferes with their flowering, indoor plants, particularly climbers, require attention in late autumn or early spring which is the time to thin out or cut back straggly growths. Depending on their style of growth, some rampant growers may also require attention during the season to keep them in check. Frequent nipping-out of the tips of new growths encourages many plants to 'break' so that they develop into bushy specimens. Left to their own devices, they could become too large and consequently worthless for their position. The style of support must be decided upon early in the life of the specimen. For some a simple wire loop may be all that is needed, others can be trained to cover a large area of wall. Plants such as some *Ficus, Monstera* and *Philodendron* will become lanky or top-heavy, eventually out-growing their position. These may be pruned back fairly hard during the spring. New growth will emerge which, before very long, develops into a useful bushy plant once more. In all staking, arrange to have the supports as unobtrusive as possible. Even the ties should not be seen; for these choose neutral colours which merge with the foliage. When pruning, care must be exercised when dealing with species which flower on their old wood, many of these require little attention. Any kinds which produce flowers on the current season's wood may be cut back after their blooms fade or very early the following season.

Propagation

Most people will make their initial plant purchases from a garden centre of florist. Having done so, it is interesting to be able to increase some of these yourself at home. The four basic methods of propagating indoor plants are from cuttings, division, layers and seed.

Cuttings of shoots, or in some cases leaves, will root when inserted in moist sand or sandy compost. Leaf cuttings of *Saintpaulia* and *Peperomia* are prepared by removing leaves complete with a portion of stem. These are inserted upright in moist sand, with the leaf-stems buried and the base of the leaf just resting on the rooting medium. *Sansevieria* leaves are cut into segments and placed upright in the pot. Some kinds of *Begonia* should have the ribs of their large leaves notched before laying the entire leaf on the surface of the pot or tray. New plantlets soon appear and may be potted up when they are large enough to handle. A periodically illuminated indoor propagator, complete with soil warming cables, is a tremendous asset in the production of new plants, especially from leaf cuttings.

Cuttings of stems should be trimmed to just below a leaf joint or node. Remove the lower leaves then dip the base of the cutting in a rooting hormone powder before inserting it into moist sandy compost. Several cuttings of smaller-growing plants can be accommodated in a pot. A plastic dome, upturned jam-jar or polythene bag secured at the pot rim will keep the atmosphere inside moist. After watering them, put the cuttings in a light position, out of the direct rays of the sun, for rooting to take place. When pale new growth reveals that the roots are forming, any covers can be removed. Once they are well rooted, the young cuttings must be potted up individually.

Usually the most convenient time for dividing up clumps to gain new plants is during the re-potting of established stock. This normally takes place in early spring. Divisions may themselves be potted up right away using fairly small pots at first. Keep the plants moist and lightly shaded until fresh roots have formed.

Layering is usually reserved for climbers, as many naturally strike root where their branches brush the soil. A modified method is used for some overgrown erect shrubs. The tips of supple-stemmed climbers can be pegged down from the large plants into small pots plunged into the soil around their base. Check their progress now and again, for in several months they should be sufficiently well rooted for severing. Allow them to continue growing in the small pots for some time before finally potting them on into good compost. To air-layer some sorts of *Philodendron* and rubber tree, remove a leaf approximately 25 cm (10 in) from the shoot tip. Next, make an upwards slanting cut well into the wood from just below to just past the bud. Wedge this split open with a matchstick and brush some rooting hormone powder into the cut before removing the wedge. A polythene sleeve, black or dark green to exclude the light, should now be secured at the top. Allow several weeks for roots to form. When they are seen pushing out from the bottom of the plastic, the stem may be severed and the new plant potted up.

Spring is seed sowing time for indoor plants. In order to raise sturdy plants, the seeds have to be well spaced over the surface of a previously moistened pot of sandy compost. After sowing, trickle some fine sand over them. If they are now covered with a piece of moist towelling material and a sheet of glass, then put into a warm dark place, there should be no need for further watering until germination. Check on progress now and then for when the tiny seedlings appear you must remove their cover and, at the same time, place the container into a diffused light situation. Be particularly careful with them at this stage, ensuring that the tiny plantlets neither dry out nor get scorched by the sun. Fine seedling compost should be used for potting on when you consider them large enough to handle.

Diseases and pests

When their cultural requirements are met, indoor plants do not as a rule suffer very much from pests or disease. As stated elsewhere, overwatering under adverse conditions is the number one killer. Correct cultivation will, to a large extent, reduce damaging physiological disorders to a minimum. Such disorders, are frequently the most difficult to identify.

Symptom Leaves dropping from the base of the plant upwards; stems thin, elongated with small leaves.
Cause Insufficient light.
Remedy Remove the plant to better light. Prune back thin stems. Water sparingly. Embark on a foliar feeding programme.

Symptom Silver-brown patches which become dark brown (dead tissue) on otherwise normal leaves.
Cause Sunburn.
Remedy Remove plant to a position out of the bright sun. This burning is common on plants when first taken outside from low light conditions. It can also occur when sunlight streams in through an unprotected window.

Symptom Tips of leaves brown.
Cause Various—most common is dry air. Under-watering, incorrect or over-feeding, coal gas and fluoride in water are all reasons for this unsightly damage.
Remedy Try to locate and correct the cause of damage, i.e. increase humidity if dry air is suspected. Trim to the edge of living tissue to remove dead portion.

Symptom Leaves pale green with often darker veining.
Cause Worn out soil or lack of feeding. Sometimes caused by lime in water.
Remedy Re-pot plant. Water with half-strength fertiliser until normal leaf colour restored.

Symptom Flower buds develop then fall before opening.
Cause Various.
Remedy Mist buds with water. Remove plants to a cooler position. Do not turn plants which are about to flower.

Symptom Plants grow well then suddenly collapse.
Cause Root rot.
Remedy No cure. Use sterilised compost. Do not overwater.
Note: Mildew which is prevalent in damp greenhouse conditions is seldom present indoors due to the dry atmosphere.

Aphid Colonies of small pale green, yellow, grey or black insects on soft growth.
Remedy Wash plant with soapy water, rinse well. Apply insecticide.

Mealy bug Small mealy-white insects with 'cotton wool'-covered eggs clustered in tight groups about the stems.
Remedy Dab insects and eggs with methylated spirit applied by cotton wool ball on end of pencil. Wash plant with soapy water, rinse well in both treatments. Once discovered, isolate your plants until pests eradicated.

Red spider mite These minute sucking pests form colonies on leaves under a fine web. This protective covering throws off plain water.

Remedy Wash the leaves in water to which a few drops of mild detergent have been added. After rinsing, spray with a suitable insecticide.

Note: Red spider mites spread rapidly under dry air conditions. They may be suspected if upper leaf surfaces become mottled with yellow. Regular misting is a good deterrent.

White fly These are first noticed when tiny white moth-like adults fly out when the plant is disturbed. The green disc-like young may be seen clustering on under-leaf surfaces.

Remedy Spray regularly with an approved insecticide if insects are seen.

Brown scale Appearing on almost any part of the plant, the brown humps of the scale insect are often found arranged along the under-leaf ribs of large-leaved plants such as *Monstera*.

Remedy Pick the insects off by hand then wash the plant down with soapy water. One or two applications of a suitable insecticide should clear up a persistent attack.

Vacation worries

'I am going away, what can I do with all my plants?' The obvious answer is to get a friend to come in to care for them, but naturally only after versing him/her well in the evils of overwatering! Failing this, many of the smaller pots can be moved to the coolest part of the house. First, give all the pots their final watering then, if they are flowering, nip off flowers and buds, for this reduces extra demand for water. A bath can be used to hold the plants. Run in a small amount of water, then stand the pots on house-bricks so that their bases are just clear of the water. If porous, these bricks will absorb water then, when it evaporates, the air around the plants will become heavily charged with moisture. Another method is to cover the plants with a polythene bag. This can be kept away from much of the foliage by inserting canes around the edge of the pot. Provided that they are left in a cool place, the plants will suffer little harm, apart from the yellowing of a few leaves.

When we go away for a short period, we prefer to plunge the pots completely into a box of moist peat or crumpled, dampened newspaper. For anyone away from their plants frequently, a good investment would be those clever self-watering pots new on the market. When filled with water or nutrient solution these keep their charges perfectly satisfied for several months, even in the summer.

Note: Throughout the Descriptions, specimens illustrated are denoted by an asterisk.

Abutilon (Malvaceae) Flowering maple

The evergreen or partly deciduous leaves of certain of this large genus are reminiscent of the typical maple-leaf in outline, hence the popular name 'Parlour maple'.

Description   In warm temperate regions, these plants, in the wild, mostly grow into large shrubs or even small trees. In cultivation, however, they withstand regular heavy pruning well and will form upright, bushy specimens. The flowers are lantern or bell-shaped, often yellow in the wild but vari-coloured in the cultivated sorts. *A. hybridum* is a race of these robust growers which includes some with variegated leaves (*A.* × *h.'Savitzii*)*. Use them as bold feature plants or foliage contrast in a mixed planter.

Cultivation   *Abutilon* are sun-lovers, developing particularly well in a sun-room or porch, minimum temperature 7°C (44°F). Keep the compost just moist at all times. Once established, generous feeding will maintain the plants' vigour and health. Dilute liquid fertiliser may be applied at 2-weekly intervals during their maximum growth period. In the spring, prune the previous season's stems to within a few centimetres of the old wood. Use a compost of equal parts of loam, peat, leaf mould and enough sand to promote free drainage. Raise young specimens from cuttings of mature wood in autumn.

Adiantum (Adiantaceae) Maidenhair ferns

This genus of nearly 200 species is of worldwide distribution. Those cultivated range from hardy alpine plants to those requiring the comfort of a constantly heated glass-house. Some members of the genus are suitable for growing indoors. Foremost among these is *A. raddianum*, also known as *A.cuneatum*. The name *Adiantum* is derived from the word *adiantos* (= dry); certain European species grow in dry places under overhanging rock ledges.

Description *A.raddianum* (Delta maidenhair)* and its several cultivars are extremely decorative indoor plants and justly popular as they are easily grown. The original species was introduced into cultivation as early as 1820. Like most other members of the genus, they can be recognised by the delicate lightness of the fronds, elegantly displayed on arching wiry black stems. In this species, the wedge-shaped leaflets, without the distinct mid-rib of most ferns, are pale green at first becoming more blue-green with age. *A.r.* 'Ocean Spray' is a very desirable cultivar of distinctive appearance. It forms an upright, shapely plant with sea-green leaflets, creased and overlapping. The fronds are dense and carried on upright black stems.

Use Maidenhair ferns either individually as table specimens or massed in a planter. The cut fronds go well with many flowers, such as carnations.

Cultivation These ferns demand plenty of light but the direct rays of the sun must not be allowed to fall upon their leaves. Additionally they need moist air, *no draughts* and a minimum temperature of 7°C (44.5°F). [It should be noted that the minimum temperatures quoted throughout mean just that, minimum meaning the lowest the plants can be reasonably expected to tolerate. Most will require considerably warmer conditions in which to flourish.] These ferns need only moderate amounts of water, with their compost kept just moist throughout the year. Plants growing indoors should be misted over occasionally, but only to freshen dusty leaves. If this operation is attended to early in the day, the warmth of the room will dry the leaves quickly; if they remain wet over night when it is cool there is a danger of the leaves becoming discoloured. An application of half-strength liquid organic fertiliser can be applied to the plants each month during the summer. Potting on is usually required annually for the first 2 to 3 years when the plants are small; use a compost rich in peat or leaf mould. If making your own compost, try using 1 part each of peat, loam and sand; add fertiliser as noted on p.12. If growth is maintained in this way, without allowing the plants to become pot-bound, some really magnificent specimens in large pots will result eventually — even under indoor conditions. Propagation is achieved by dividing up the crowns of old plants or by sowing spores. This is an easy operation if one owns a glass-house, where they sometimes seed themselves, and not impossible for the window-sill gardener.

Aechmaea (Bromeliaceae)

This genus of some 150, mostly epiphytic, species contains some of the most ornamental indoor plants that we have.

Description The attraction of this group lies both in the rosette of sword-like leaves, arranged to form a water-retaining cup, and in the upright or arching flower spikes. These are often followed by clustered, coloured berries which last for weeks. *A. fasciata* (Silver vase)* is one of the more popular kinds with broad, leathery, dull green leaves, bearing a showy inflorescence of bright pink bracts and blue flowers. This combination of handsome leaves, together with regular, long-lasting flowering, makes this species one of the more familiar of the group. Use them as free-standing floor specimens, to decorate a low table or, when out of flower, as foliage plants in a mixed grouping.

Cultivation Provided weather conditions are warm, *Aechmaea* grow best in a moderate to bright light. Also, having regard to their Brazilian tropical rain forest origins, they are easiest to grow in a humid atmosphere. For optimum growth, a temperature of 16°C (61°F) or more is desirable. A useful tip to protect the plants from severe damage in dull wintry weather is to empty their 'cups' of collected moisture. Having done this, the plants will tolerate temperatures as low as 5°C (41°F). As these are plants which require a constantly moist air, they will need frequent watering. In spite of this they detest wet compost. Bear in mind that these are epiphytes which, in the wild, live on the atmosphere as they cluster in the forks of trees or develop on mounds of fallen bark. Naturally rain water is best to use and the leaves should be sprayed frequently during hot weather. Prior to feeding, their leaf reservoirs should be flushed out with clean water, then half-strength liquid organic fertiliser should be applied to both cup and compost. Feeding is only needed for a few months during the plants' peak season of growth. Smaller pots than their size otherwise indicates should be used. A porous, rather acid compost of granulated peat, leaf mould and shredded fir bark will be sufficient to anchor the plants. We get good results from using an orchid mix for this whole group. Propagation is effected by severing the offsets produced by the dying flowering rosette. This may be done the following summer or when they have developed at least five good leaves.

It may be necessary to strip off the outer leaves in order to expose sufficient area for roots to form. Pot them up, using small pots, into a compost of moist peat and sand. Keep them close — i.e. in a moist atmosphere, in light but out of direct sun. Transfer the young plants to larger pots with a coarse compost during the following spring. Brown leaf ends indicate too dry an atmosphere. Larger dead areas mean either that the compost is too wet or that the temperature is intolerably low. If leaves are elongated, the plants require more light.

Aglaonema (Araceae) Chinese evergreen

This is a genus of about 20 species of evergreen perennials from the tropics, many of which are grown for the attractiveness of their patterned leaves. Their Latin name comes from *aglaos* (= bright) and *nema* (= thread), perhaps from the flower's shining stamens. Despite their name, only one species, the first to be introduced, actually originated in China. Others are wild plants of Malaya, Thailand, Burma and parts of the East Indies. Several garden-raised forms are an improvement on the original species.

Description   Chinese evergreens have smooth leaves, often glossy, ovate or lanceolate, pointed, arranged in a dense cluster. The arum-like inflorescence is of secondary importance as far as decorative value is concerned. The tiny yellow or white flowers are crowded on a club-shaped spadix; the spathe becomes elongated after fertilisation. Later, clustered red berries may appear. *A.commutatum* has dark green pointed leaves marked wtih areas of paler green and silver. *A.c.maculatum** is a natural variant with its less pointed leaves boldly marked in silvery white. *A.c.* 'Albo-variegatum' is a cultivar raised as a sport in the USA. Its green and white leaves are carried on contrasting white stems. *A.costatum* (Spotted evergreen) is a smaller-grower originally found in Malaysia. This species bears glossy oval leaves, well marked with white and with a white mid-rib. *A.crispum* (Painted drop tongue, Pewter plant) is a robust-grower with its evergreen leaves shaded silver-grey. *A.* 'Fransher' (*A.treubii* × *marantifolium tricolor*) is a valuable hybrid with a slender habit of growth. Its long oval green leaves are 'feathered' in cream and held on white stems. *A.modestum* (Chinese evergreen) has stalked, long-lasting, leathery, ovate blue-green leaves, somewhat pendant, on erect stems. *A.* 'Silver King' is a robust hybrid with its long, oval, dark green leaves virtually obscured by a silvered surface. Chinese evergreens are particularly valued as room plants for their low-light tolerance. Because of this they may be placed, along with ferns, in positions where few flowering plants can survive. They also do well under total artificial light. Use these plants as individual specimens on a table or shelf, in groups, or in a glass-covered terrarium.

Cultivation   The ability that these plants have to thrive under low light conditions enables them to be grown in the shade with a minimum temperature of 10°C (50°F). Water the pots only when the compost surface feels dry, then give them a good soaking, allowing the pots to drain through before replacing them in their covers. The leaves may be misted over under hot, dry air conditions. These are not gross feeders; a monthly application of dilute liquid manure is sufficient. No feeding is required during the winter. Select an open loamy compost for potting. Re-potting may be needed every other year. Propagation is by division of the rooted stems or cuttings of the basal shoots. The latter method needs the close humid conditions of the propagating case in order to succeed with any degree of certainty.

Alocasia (Araceae)

Although demanding a specialised type of care, this genus of tropical arads, numbering about 60 species, will repay any amount of attention as they display their magnificent boldly patterned and attractively shaped leaves. First and foremost one has to remember that the original home of these vigorous growing herbaceous plants is in the steaming jungles of Asia. Therefore constant damp and heat (obviously no draughts!) is needed for the leaves to develop to their full potential. Naturally enough, where the plants grow, the weather is not as constant or as perfect for them all the time as one may imagine. Sudden wet squally showers, torrential rain — even cool nights, can occur. The plants use their built-in adaptability to survive. They can even do this under certain indoor conditions. The name *Alocasia* is a variation of *Calocasia,* a closely related genus under which all of these plants were originally listed. Other near relatives are the very beautiful *Caladium*. It is reported that, in their native haunts, the roots of *Alocasia* are cooked and eaten and, being starchy, they are nutritious. The leaves are prepared and used much as we use spinach.

Description As cultivated plants, these are of surprisingly rapid growth but only when the conditions are right. The often large leaves, supported on stout stems, are arrow- or heart-shaped, with veins clearly picked out in a contrasting colour. *A.cuprea* is a suitable species to grow indoors. Found wild in Borneo, it bears bronze-purple leaves, paler beneath and with markedly depressed veins. *A.lindenii* is a compact grower, having its slender, pointed, heart-shaped leaves coloured shining green with white veins. *A.sanderiana** has showy arrow-shaped leaves with the deeply lobed margins bordered in white. The upper leaf surface is smooth, silver-green, the veins white or yellow.

Use these bold foliage plants in indoor gardens to provide a genuine tropical effect. Water is a natural feature and plants will benefit from the micro-climate it provides.

Cultivation As noted previously, these handsome foliage plants need extra care if they are to succeed. Place them in the shade with a minimum (winter) temperature of 16°C (61°F). In a suitable environment, abundant water should be given throughout the growing season and drier air and compost during their winter rest. Liquid feed, using suitably diluted organic-based fertiliser, once each week while the plants are in active growth. For potting use a mixture of peat, loam, leaf mould and well-rotted manure in equal parts with enough sand to promote free drainage. Start the growth off in the spring by increasing the heat and water but still allowing the compost around the tuberous roots to dry partially between waterings. Later, when the leaves unfurl, more water may be given. Propagate your plants by division or removing offsets during the spring. A heated glass-house is almost a necessity for propagation and a great advantage for overwintering the established pots.

Anthurium (Araceae) Tail flower

This is a very large genus containing about 500 species, all evergreen and all natives of tropical America. Both botanical and common names amount to the same, for *anthos* means flower, and *oure* means tail; hence Tail flower. Many species are natually epiphytic in the wild, growing in the clefts of trees or, more often, in the fallen debris of the forest floor. Rather surprisingly they take well to normal pot culture, provided of course that their other requirements are met and adhered to. Unfortunately, unless *Anthurium* receive the correct amount of warmth and moisture, they are difficult to maintain in a satisfactory manner when kept entirely in an indoor situation.They will grow well in the modern equivalent of a Wardian case — a glazed indoor structure with heating and lighting linked to the special need of the plants it contains — or for short periods alternating between greenhouse and indoors.

Description   *A.scherzerianam* (Painter's palette, Flamingo or Flame flower) in one of its cultivar forms is probably the kind familiar to the majority of people and is also the most satisfactory sort for growing indoors. A native of Costa Rica, this species was introduced into Britain *via* Germany by H. W. Gower in the year 1861. Before very long, many different varieties came on to the market. A compact clump-forming plant, it has thick, leathery, dark green elliptic leaves which end in a long tapering point. The inflorescence consists of an elongated spathe which, in the original species, is a uniform rich scarlet with a contrasting, slightly curled, orange-yellow spadix. The spathe is persistent, lasting several months on the plant. The flowers are produced intermittently from the spring through until the autumn. *A.andreanum* (Tail flower)* has heart-shaped leaves and magnificent scarlet spathes. High humidity is a must for these beautiful plants.

Use these plants in mixed groups in the indoor garden where the close proximity of other plants tends to produce the humid micro-climate that they need.

Cultivation   Light shade coupled with constant even warmth,as well as high humidity, are the requirements for these plants with their spectacular flowers. The minimum temperature is 16°C (61°F). From spring to autumn, the pots require frequent watering as well as overhead spraying; use naturally warm rainwater for both operations. Keep the roots barely moist during the plants' winter dormancy period. Being naturally forest-dwellers, they require little food apart from that in their compost, particularly if the compost is high in humus-forming materials. A dilute solution of dried blood in water may be given to flowering plants if desired. A compost of peat and leaf mould in equal parts with shredded fir bark *or* chopped fresh sphagnum moss, to keep the material open and well aerated, will be best for these plants. Increase your stock by sowing freshly gathered seeds. Alternatively the clumps may be divided, taking care to avoid damaging their brittle roots. The latter method is of course essential for named sorts and should be done during the winter.

Aphelandra (Acanthaceae) Zebra plant

This is a large genus of nearly 200 species of tropical American shrubs. The cultivated species have glossy, often variegated leaves and spikes of brilliantly coloured flowers.

Description A.*aurantiaca* (Fiery spike)* forms an erect shrubby plant with silvered, dull green, ovate leaves and short spikes of scarlet bracts, together with orange-throated flowers. A.*squarrosa* (Zebra plant), from Brazil, bears lustrous evergreen leaves, heavily veined in contrasting colour, which prompted their common name. The impressive flower heads comprise a four-sided spike in which both bracts and tubular flowers are brightly coloured. This species, popular with indoor plant growers is usually represented in our homes by one of its cultivars. Both 'Dania' and 'Louisae' have wide white veining on their narrow, dark green leaves, together with extra showy flowers. The original species has narrow elliptic leaves with mid-rib and veins picked out in white. Both species and cultivars normally bear a number of inflorescences, rich golden-yellow in colour with the bracts red-edged in some sorts. The flower heads are pyramidal in outline, tapering to the base with projecting two-lipped yellow flowers.

Use them for an individual display or in a mixed planting where, even out of flower, they remain an attraction. Although providing a splendid display during their first season, these plants are not really long-term or easily grown room plants.

Cultivation Zebra plants require good light but, at the same time, need to be shaded from the hot sun, which tends to cause the leaf edges to brown. Minimum temperature is 12°C (53.5°F). Pots should be kept just moist throughout the year. Feed the plants regularly at 2-weekly intervals during the growing season, monthly at other times. After flowering, the plants can be given a partial rest by reducing the amount of water given. This must never be so little as to cause any shrivelling of the evergreen leaves. This short period of rest is beneficial to plants and will result in a better start the following season. Growth restarts in late winter when a higher temperature, together with an occasional overhead misting, is needed. Prune at this time by removing the weak shoots altogether and pruning back the strongest to two or three leaf joints above the pot rim. This treatment ensures dwarf, stocky specimens. Annual re-potting into fresh compost may be done when the new shoots, which will form the current year's plants, are developing. Make certain that the pots are clean when re-potting, for these plants are particularly susceptible to root rots brought about by unsterile conditions.

Contrary to normal practice, it is not advisable to pinch out the growing points to encourage bushiness, for the stronger these early shoots develop the larger the leaves and better the flowering spikes will be. A suitable compost can be made up from good loam, peat and leaf mould in equal parts with sufficient coarse sand added to ensure sharp drainage. *Aphelandra* are propagated by inserting half-ripe shoots in moist sand during the spring. Obtain these from previously pruned plants, utilising only those which are not required to form the flowering growths.

Araucaria (Araucariaceae) Norfolk Island pine

Of the hundreds of kinds of conifers in existence, surprisingly few make good indoor plants. In such a situation they tend to shed their leaves almost as soon as they are brought inside. Of this genus, which contains 18 species, there is one, *A.heterophylla**, which is perfectly amenable to cultivation in the home.

Description   When grown naturally, *A.heterophylla* develop into tall, straight trees of 60 m (200 ft) with wide-spreading branches; when young they are most attractive in a pot. Their leaves are closely set, on whorled branches, awl-shaped, soft to the touch, a light fresh green when young, becoming dark green with age. This species, together with the other members of the genus, is native to several countries bordering the Pacific Ocean. Use them as individuals or as the centre of a large planter where they will best develop their pyramidal outline.

Cultivation   Grow in an airy position, with good light and part shade when hot. These slow-growing pot plants will withstand a minimum temperature of 5°C (41°F). Sometimes their leaves collect dust, a situation which can be remedied by placing the pots outside during a light shower for the rain to freshen them up. Any well drained compost which is kept just moist will suit them. When re-potting, the old root-ball should be placed scarcely deeper in the new pot than it was previously. Long-term specimen plants require feeding just as much, if not more, than younger ones and, for these, foliar feeding sprays are very useful as they may be simply misted over the leaves. Alternatively, try making several holes with a pencil in the surface of the compost, up to a finger's length deep, according to the size of the pot. Sprinkle some fertiliser granules into these holes and plug them with fresh compost.

Propagation is from seed or tip cuttings. The latter is a highly specialised process unlikely to be attempted except by one or two nurserymen in the world and then only to increase cultivars of the Norfolk Island pine such as *A.h.* 'Gracilis'. This sort appears to be more graceful than the type because of its narrow leaves. To the uninitiated buyer in Britain, at first glance these could appear to be particularly good, perhaps greenhouse grown (if there were such a thing!), specimens of *Picea excelsa*, the Christmas tree.

Asparagus (Liliaceae)

This is a large genus of evergreen plants native to southern Africa, several of which are suited to indoor culture.

Description   These plants have no 'true' leaves in the normal sense of the word for their foliage consists of phylloclades, modified branchlets; the leaves, if they exist at all, are in the hooks used by some species for climbing. The phylloclades, always tiny, are very numerous, giving our house plants a particularly light and dainty appearance. The insignificant flowers are sometimes followed by shining red berries which, incidently, are much beloved by Blackbirds, *Turdus merula,* in countries where these birds are native or introduced. *A. densiflora* is a South African species normally represented in cultivation by two cultivars, which are often considered as 'good' species. *A.d.* 'Myersii' (syn. *A.myersii,* Plume asparagus) has upright or slightly arching stems encircled with dense, at first soft, needle-like leaves, each plumose branch tapering towards the tip. *A.d.* 'Sprengerii' (syn. *A.sprengerii*)* is a familiar indoor plant, the branches of which grow from tuberous roots. Their foliage consists of fresh green, flattened needle-like phylloclades massed on cascading stems. Given space to develop, this plant will climb a support, such as a trellis, by means of its sharp recurved hooks. *A.setaceous* (syn. *A.plumosus,* Asparagus fern) produces its soft, bright green, bristle-like needles in horizontally branched layers. As the plants mature, the stiff green stems often elongate, also developing a climbing manner of growth. This is the 'fern' of the florists' bouquets.

Use these easy-to-grow plants as individuals in baskets, either alone or as a centre-piece for other flowers.

Cultivation   Although able to cope with varying amounts of light, the ideal conditions for the ornamental asparagus is what gardeners term a 'buoyant' atmosphere, i.e. warm and damp but without stagnant humidity, and with a temperature of 10°C (50°F). Do not overwater these plants at any time; rather allow the compost surface to become dry between each watering. An overhead misting with a fine atomiser during spells of particularly hot weather will keep the foliage clean and fresh. Rich sandy loam compost suits them well. Make this up yourself from 3 parts good loam, 2 parts moist peat or seived leaf mould and 1 part sand plus a small quantity of fertiliser. Increase your plants by dividing up the dense crowns during the early spring or by sowing seed. The latter method is much to be preferred, for amateur growers are frequently guilty of causing the demise of certain plants by their over-enthusiastic breaking up of unsuitable material. Pruning consists of cutting out any dead or poor thin shoots completely.

Asplenium (Aspleniaceae) Spleenwort

This very large genus of ferns contains somewhere between 600 and 700 species. They are of worldwide distribution in both tropical and temperate regions. Their botanical name comes from *a* (= not) and *splen,* (= spleen), apparently in reference to the former use of certain European sorts as a curative for disorders of the spleen. They are popular with growers of indoor plants and gardeners in general because they are evergreen and because they are so diverse in form.

Description *Asplenium* are tufted in growth, the fronds developing from either one or several crowns. The fronds vary in shape according to the species, from undivided to extremely cut and of feathery appearance. Unlike the deciduous ferns, their leaf texture is firm and the fronds long-lasting. *A.bulbiferum* (Hen and chickens fern) is found growing naturally in Australasia and Malaysia. These plants eventually develop stout crowns from which the well feathered fronds arch outwards, gracefully supported on stout wiry black stalks. Their common name stems from the fact that the leaf axils produce numerous round bulbils which eventually develop into clusters of leaves. A mature frond which, under ideal conditions, would be as long as 1 m (3¼ ft), has the appearance of being almost overcome by the weight of these tufts. If detached and placed in a pot or box of sandy peat, they soon root and offer a ready means of increasing your plants. *A.nidus* (syn. *A.nidus-avis,* Bird's nest fern)* comes from South-East Asia and tropical Australia. In the wild it is an epiphyte, flourishing in the forks of trees or around their bases. The plant consists of a rosette of undivided, leathery, fresh green leaves, reminiscent of a shuttlecock in shape when they are young. As each leaf uncurls from the centre it elongates and develops upwards and outwards to leave a central well. A mass of aerial roots forms over the pot surface and these draw sustenance from the surrounding air, so that very little compost is required.

Cultivation Spleenwort ferns prefer a diffused light to shade although they do tolerate the latter. Minimum temperature is 10°C (50°F). Ample water should be given during the spring and summer months, at which time naturally warm rain water may be poured into the 'nests' of *A.nidus* fronds. The compost in which *A.bulbiferum* plants are grown should be kept moist at all times. Unfortunately *A.nidus* crowns rot easily if too much water is given when the temperature is low. A light misting over of the foliage will maintain them in good condition during cooler times. Little feeding is needed for these, if at all. For ferns, some people feed monthly with half-strength fertiliser. The compost for potting should be mildly acid with a high humus content. Use a mixture of leaf mould, peat and sand with perhaps some fibrous loam. Our little plant grows happily in finely rubbed leaf mould from beneath a pine tree. This kind can be increased by sowing spores. Hen and chickens fern grows easily and rapidly from bulbils.

Begonia (Begoniaceae)

This large genus contains several distinct groups, including succulent herbaceous perennials and sub-shrubs which are normally fibrous- or rhizomatous-rooted and sorts with tuberous roots. The majority of plants we see are garden-raised hybrids. *Begonia* are natives of various moist tropical regions of the world (excluding Australasia).

Description   These plants are of diverse appearance, some tall with cane-like stems, others dwarf, flowers and/or foliage being their individual main feature. Their leaves are alternate, more or less unequal-sided, earning for some the popular name 'Elephants' ears'. These leaves can be lobed or toothed as well as entire, glossy or hairy — some splendidly coloured. *B.* × *cheimantha* (Lorraine or Christmas begonia), a group of hybrids developed from the original crosses between *B.dreigi* and *B.socotrana,* form extremely floriferous upright bushy specimens with clusters of small flowers in a good colour range. 'Gloire de Lorraine' is the original hybrid raised in France by the nursery firm of Lemoine of Nancy. It carries abundant, tiny four-petalled pink blooms above the rather brittle, fresh green leaves. *B.* 'Cleopatra' is a useful hybrid cherished for its pretty foliage. The leaves are thin, almost transparent, light green with brown blotches. The plants develop creeping rhizomes and new stems covered in white hairs. Branched heads of pale pink blooms appear during late summer. *B.* 'Corallina de Lucerna' (Spotted angelwing begonia) develops tall woody stems with semi-drooping dark green leaves flushed red beneath. The upper leaf surface is polka-dotted with a mass of silver spots. The bunches of clear pink flowers are borne in pendant clusters, making this an all-round, taller, indoor flowering plant which is attractive either in or out of flower. *B.* × *erythrophylla* (Beefsteak begonia) and *B.manicata* × *hydocotyfolia* are interesting plants primarily on account of the large leathery, rounded leaves. These are carried on strong fleshy stems, deep shining green above, red below. The generous clusters of pale pink or white blooms (the intensity of the colour appears to depend on their exposure to light) are held well above the leaves. *B.* × *hiemalis* (Winter-flowering begonia) is a valuable group of hybrids between *B. socotrana* and various summer-flowering tuberous sorts. They develop into upright bushy plants with large, thin, dark green leaves and stems of clustered, saucer-shaped flowers which nestle into the top of the domed plants. The recently introduced German strain of Reiger's 'Elatior' hybrids* are particularly fine. These have blooms in colours ranging from white, yellow and apricot to scarlet and bronze, each with a central boss of complementary golden stamens. *B. masoniana* (Iron cross begonia), is a superb foliage plant from South-East Asia introduced into cultivation *via* Singapore. The silver-grey leaves are bristly with a puckered surface, the central area clearly marked with a brown iron-cross-like pattern. *B. rex* (Fan begonia)* is another race of fine foliage plants. Those we grow are hybrids of the original Indian species and develop their leaves from thick, below-surface rhizomes. The stalks are red and hairy and the variously shaped leaves are coloured and marked in a multitude of different patterns. Many received individual cultivar names in the past. The pale rose flowers of older specimens are an attraction in themselves. *B. semperflorens* (Wax begonia) is a virtually continuously flowering plant developed from a Brazilian species. Individually these are small and bushy with thick, upright, succulent stems and leaves. The latter can be green to deep bronze-purple in colour. The flowers are pink, red, mauve or white — either single or double. Several seed-raised strains are available for summer bedding out. They can be potted up after their normal season ends to make a further bright showing on a sunlit

Begonia (Begoniaceae) *cont'd*

window-sill during the winter months. The named sorts developed for indoor use are better. Their tiny, fully double, rosebud-like blooms are particularly charming. *B.* × *tuberhybrida* (Tuberous begonia)* has thick watery-stemmed growths, which die right down after flowering. Tubers bought in spring should be pushed into pots of moist peat compost. Provide early support for the brittle stems. To make the gorgeous fleshy flowers even larger let only one stem develop from a tuber, feed regularly, and remove female flowers from the side of the main bud.

Cultivation Diffused sunlight to part shade is preferred by plants of this genus and a minimum temperature of 10°C (50°F). Their growing medium must be constantly just moist, with more water being given when they are in active growth or flowering. Surrounding high humidity is preferable to syringing over the leaves. Established plants can be fed by utilising a liquid formulation during the spring/summer or side-dressing with time-release capsules at the start of the season. For potting up, use either a mixture of loam, peat and sand or a soil-less preparation. In some kinds, new plants come from leaf cuttings. Others can be increased from seeds, cuttings or by cutting up a pre-sprouted dry tuber.

Beloperone (Acanthaceae) Shrimp plant

Description Of this genus of evergreen shrubs from tropical America, *B.guttata* (Shrimp plant)* is an easily grown plant of only recent introduction, with colourful, quaint shrimp-like inflorescences, composed of overlapping, papery, reddish-brown bracts, almost hiding tiny, white tubular flowers. These plants are virtually continuously in bloom. The leaves are soft green, ovate in outline, and are carried on rather brittle stems. *B.g.* 'Yellow Queen' is a valuable addition to the original 1936 introduction and displays clear yellow bracts. Use Shrimp plants individually for a novelty display of bright colour.

Cultivation Although some shade is tolerated, the best flower colour is seen when the plants are grown in a relatively sunny position, minimum temperature 10°C (50°F). Watering can be frequent during active growth. Feeding at this time, with a weekly application of soluble fertiliser, promotes stems clad with lush leaves, together with masses of flower heads. When growth has slowed, partially with-hold water, allowing the compost to become nearly dry each time. Either a standard loam-based or loam-less compost can be used for these. The little shrubs are naturally bushy but the old flower stems should be removed occasionally. A light trim during late winter is advisable to keep the plants looking shapely and to retain their vigour. These are not long-lived, so a few tip cuttings rooted in sand during the early summer will provide stock for the future.

Billbergia (Bromeliaceae)

Named in honour of the Swedish botanist, J. G. Billberg (1772–1844), this genus from South America comprises over 50 species. They are easy to grow yet among the showiest of the bromeliads. *Billbergia* are similar to the closely related *Aechmaea*, both in appearance and cultivation requirements, although they are generally more hardy. Indeed several kinds can tolerate near freezing temperatures for a short period of time when they are resting.

Description The leaves of *Billbergia* are rigid, arranged in clustered rosettes. They can be wide or rolled into a tube and, in the cultivars of some species, are attractively marbled or banded*. The flowers, which appear during the autumn or winter, are also attractive, often spectacular. *B.nutans* (Queen's or Angel's tears) was introduced to horticultural circles in Britain during the year 1868. It is a clump-forming species with elongated, almost tubular, rosettes of stiff dark green leaves, liberally dusted with silvery scales. Plants which are grown in sunny windows adopt a reddish sheen to their leaves. The long, arching flower stems are pink, as are the bracts. The hanging flowers are pale green, edged in violet, The common name of these attractive plants is derived from the fact that a 'teardrop' of moisture is frequently present on the tip of the protruding stigma.

These plants make fine specimens for a low table where their decorative leaves are a feature, even when the plants are out of flower.

Cultivation *Billbergia* adapt readily to indoor situations where they prefer a light position; shade results in a loss of good leaf colour. A place where they perhaps receive full light for the winter months and then diffused sunlight for the remainder of the year will be ideal. Minimum temperature is 10°C (50°F). When watering, see that the rosette 'cup' formed by the leaves is frequently topped up with water and the compost just moist. Spray the leaves daily if need be, during particularly hot weather. Feeding with half-strength organic liquid fertiliser may be done at monthly intervals during the active growing season. The cups, as well as the compost, should both receive their share of plant food. The potting compost used for the epiphytes should comprise 1 part each of peat or leaf mould, acid loam and shredded bark or perlite. Experience shows that this whole group detests both soggy and hard compost, so ensure that your potting medium is open and free-draining. Plants of this genus normally produce numerous offsets which may be readily used to perpetuate your stock of plants. As these develop best whilst still nurtured by the parent there should be no rush to detach them. Rather allow them to attain at least one-third of their ultimate size before removing them with a twisting movement of the wrist. The base should be trimmed and the outer leaves removed altogether before inserting the 'pups' into pots of very sandy peat. Keep them in a warm partly shaded place for about 3-4 weeks before allowing them more light and moisture. Many plants will constantly produce offsets which demand considerable thinning if the clumps are to remain healthy and attractive.

Blechnum (Blechnaceae)

This large genus contains between 180 and 200 species from temperate and tropical regions. They vary from creeping alpines to handsome, highly decorative specimens of strong habit. Their name comes from *blechnon,* the Greek word for fern.

Description Most indoor plants from this genus have large arching fronds which are either pinnate (divided to the rachis or mid-rib rather like a bird's feather) or pinnatifid (nearly, but not quite, cut into separate pinnae). *B.gibbum** is a particularly attractive fern at all stages of development. Although it may become very large, with a well developed, trunk-like stem, this New Caledonian species will make an admirable specimen for a shaded spot in a warm room for many years. The arching fronds are clad with leathery, narrow, shining green pinnae.

Cultivation This splendid tropical species needs a draught-free, warm, shady position, minimum temperature 12°C (53.5°F). High humidity rather than abundant water is the rule but the compost must not be allowed to dry out. Use half-strength liquid fertiliser at 2-monthly intervals. For compost use peat, leaf mould and sandy loam. Pot the plants fairly loosely in their containers. New plants come from tiny spores, an impractical means of increasing stock for the indoor gardener.

Brunfelsia (Solanaceae)

This genus of evergreen shrubs from the West Indies and tropical America was named by Plumier in honour of Otto Brunfels. Unfortunately, they are not among the easiest of indoor plants to grow due primarily to dry air.

Description *B.calycina** is a low-growing shrub with upright branches which eventually develops into a spreading bush. The elliptic leaves are glossy green with a leathery texture. The scented flowers appear from spring to early summer and intermittently at other times. They are borne in clusters and open in succession. They are long-tubed, with five large petals, lasting in colour for three days — hence the name Yesterday, today and tomorrow! Each petal is wavy-edged, the flowers opened out flat and violet-blue in colour, fading to lavender.

Cultivation Light shade is required in bright weather and constant high humidity. Minimum temperature 12°C (53.5°F). Spray the leaves with tepid water in warm weather, especially if the plants are making new growth. Keep the compost constantly just moist but never really wet. Water with a weak dilution of liquid manure monthly from spring until autumn. When re-potting make up a compost of loam, leaf mould and peat in equal parts and add a little silver sand to keep the mixture open. Cuttings 'strike' when taken during the spring.

Caladium (Araceae)

This genus comprises some 16 species of tuberous-rooted herbaceous plants.

Description *C.hortulanum* (Fancy-leaf caladium)* includes a number of garden-raised kinds derived mainly from *C.bicolor,* a stocky, deciduous, parti-coloured leaf plant. The wafer-thin leaves, mostly broad, heart-shaped, or arrow- or strap-shaped, sometimes with a crinkled surface or margin, are held on slender stems. Their incredible colouring and delicate translucence are outstanding: red, pink, bronze, yellow and white, with veins or spots either in self colours or contrasting in a riotous medley of rose and scarlet. Unfortunately they are not the easiest of plants to grow or maintain.

Cultivation *Caladium* revel in moist heat — and definitely dislike draughts. Good light is essential to bring out the best leaf colouration. Care is needed to prevent sun-scorch, particularly if the air is dry; a year round temperature of 15-18°C (59-64.5°F) is required. Start the tubers into growth in early spring; water the pots sparingly at first. Later, when growth is more advanced, more generous amounts can be given. Start weekly liquid feeds once the first leaves are unfurled. A very well drained compost should be used, of loam, well rotted manure and sand. Increase by careful division of the flattish tubers early in the year. Place a single crown in each pot.

Calathea (Marantaceae)

This genus contains well over 100 species of tropical South American plants. The cultivated kinds are generally of tufted growth with the leaf blades coloured and beautifully marked. The name *Calathea* was probably derived from the Greek *kalathos* (=basket).

Description *C.mackoyana* (Peacock plant)* is a dwarf-grower with comparatively large upright leaves, oval in shape, and coloured and marked most attractively. They are greenish-yellow above, with contrasting dark green veins; large and small spots or blotches of black also decorate the upper leaf surface. The under-leaf is pale red patterned with deep wine-red. These plants are exacting and cannot be classed as easy or even moderately easy to grow indoors. They do have a use, albeit a rather special one — in 'jungle' jars, those large glass containers, where, with the even warmth plus high humidity, they flourish.

Cultivation A position with filtered sunlight should be selected, minimum temperature 15°C (59°F). A moderate amount of water is needed to keep the compost moist throughout each season. Liquid feed may be applied at 2-weekly intervals from spring to summer. A humus-rich compost containing plenty of leaf mould is needed. New plants can be obtained by careful division of the crowns during the summer; keep these shaded until enough new roots have formed.

Campanula (Campanulaceae) Bell flower

Although this huge family contains many notable garden plants, very few are suited for growing indoors. *C.isophylla* (Star of Bethlehem)* from Italy is an exception.

Description These have pendant stems, bearing grey-green, ovate leaves; towards the ends develop masses of open, star-like, pale blue flowers. They bloom from spring well into summer. Use these charming, easily grown subjects in a cool inside window or hanging basket.

Cultivation As these plants are virtually hardy they require ample light without too much heat. An upper temperature limit of around 20°C (68°F) is advised. Higher temperatures are acceptable if the humidity is increased accordingly. Water the pots well to keep the compost moist during the growing season. Later, as the growth slows, reduce the amount given, allowing the compost to become partially dry each time. A loam-based soil containing a proportion of chalk (ground limestone) or standard potting compost will suit these plants well. Weekly light feeding may be undertaken during the spring flush of growth. The plants must be clipped over in late winter to ensure vigorous new flowering stems. Propagate by division of the crowns very early in the year or by rooting soft cuttings, each of which should be detached with a tiny piece of old stem.

Ceropegia (Asclepiadaceae) Lantern flower

Ceropegia contains about 150 species. *C.woodii** (Heart vine, Chain of hearts, String of hearts) from Natal, South Africa, is a novelty indoor plant and of decorative value because of its completely pendant manner of growth.

Description These are tuberous-rooted plants. From these roots, long, thin, purple stems are produced. Each carries many pairs of small, stalked, fleshy, broadly heart-shaped leaves, dark green in colour and heavily marbled in silver-grey. The tiny flowers which, in an established plant, appear in the leaf nodes, open in succession. They are pinkish purple in colour, brown within. Sometimes small tubers also appear on the plants' thread-like stems. They can be detached when large enough, put in a pot filled with potting mix, and in a short time, you have a tiny plant to give to a friend. (This is how we received ours!)

Cultivation The strings of leaves develop best when the plants are placed high up in a semi-lit position, out of full sunlight. They are particularly frost-tender; minimum temperature of 16°C (61°F). Water freely during hot weather but, in cooler conditions, give less water so the compost becomes virtually dry. This treatment will result in larger, more succulent leaves of better colour. Use a compost of equal parts of screened leaf mould and peat plus sharp sand. Propagate by shoot tip cuttings in summer or by nodules.

Chlorophytum (Liliaceae) Spider plant

The Latin name for these popular, easily grown plants is derived from *chloros* (=green) and *phyton* (=plant). The individuals we grow in our homes are, however, almost invariably the variegated sports.

Description *Chlorophytum* are evergreen, tuberous-rooted herbaceous plants with soft (more rigid at the base), narrow, grass-like leaves which arch outwards from the centre of the clump. Over 200 species have been recorded. *C.comosum* 'Vittatum'* is a favourite originating from Natal, South Africa. It displays long, narrow, strap-shaped leaves which are loosely arranged in a rosette. Individually these leaves are channelled, each stripe with a wide central band of white. Even longer are the branched, wiry, flower stems. These bear starry white blooms which, in turn, are followed by tufts of leaves. Aerial roots develop later and the surplus can be detached and potted up, thus forming a ready means of increase. This species is most interesting from the point of view of its viviparous habit of producing plantlets on the ends of the former flowering stems in this manner.

When Spider plants are placed in a basket or on a pedestal*, their offspring drape around the main plant in a most attractive way.

Cultivation *Chlorophytum* spp. are easily grown, almost hardy plants, thriving indoors in temperatures as low as 7°C (44.5°F) or less. They may be displayed in a light place but do beware of the sun scorching their leaves. Moderate amounts of water are required when the plants are in active growth, little or just sufficient to stop the compost shrinking away from the pot rim at other times. Liquid feeding at monthly intervals will supplement the fertiliser incorporated in the compost. These plants, although of only moderate ultimate size, are vigorous growers, needing a rich soil in order to maintain a healthy appearance. A suitable mix for these should comprise 3 parts turfy loam, 1 part granulated peat, 1 part well-rotted manure and 1 part sharp sand, together with added fertiliser at the rate of approximately 2 tablespoons per bucket of mixed compost. In addition to rooting their offsets, the plants may be increased by separating the crowns during the spring. Browning of the leaf tips indicates either too dry an atmosphere or lack of water at the roots, which occurs when the clumps require splitting and re-potting.

48

Cineraria (Compositae)

Cineraria *(Senecio cruentus)* * is part of the great genus of groundsels (see also p. 156). Although formerly called American groundsels, they are in fact African in origin, with the main parent found as a wilding in the Canary Islands. These are perennials, usually treated as annuals when grown in greenhouses. They are then, as are several other plants (see below), brought indoors for a very showy, even if somewhat temporary, display.

Cultivated cinerarias are compact with bold, rounded, glossy green leaves against which the flattened clusters of pink, red, orange or purple daisy-like flowers are displayed to perfection. Place these plants in good light. Cool conditions prolong the flowering. Water when the compost feels dry.

Other temporary indoor flowering pot plants These form a valuable addition to the permanent plants that we grow in our homes. Produced solely to create instant colour when and where it is needed, most are prepared for winter and spring sales. Some are greenhouse annuals and perennials; others are hardy and tropical shrubs. Again, the frequency of watering is the most misunderstood aspect of their cultural requirement. If in doubt, allow the pots to become partially dry before giving them a thorough soak. When selecting plants choose stocky, well-branched specimens with nice plump leaves. If they are actually flowering at the time of purchase, make certain that there are more unopened buds to follow. As well as watering problems, frost and draughts are to be avoided if good value for money is to be obtained.

Azaleas *(Rhododendron simsii)* are bushy evergreen shrubs. Many superb sorts have been raised in cultivation since their first introductions from China. When flowering, the blooms, in shades of red, pink, magenta and white, are so dense as to obscure the foliage completely. Cool, humid conditions and a position out of direct sunlight will prolong their usefulness. Never let their compost of rotted pine needles or peat dry out but use rain water to keep it moist at all times. Feed every 2 weeks, especially if it is intended to bed them out in a shady spot when frosts are over.

Calceolaria × *herbeo-hybrida* (Slipper flower) is a group of exotic-looking biennials with masses of large pouched flowers in shades of red and yellow. Grow these in diffused light and water the pots when the surface feels dry.

Chrysanthemums form dwarf plants with masses of blooms in white, yellow, pink, bronze etc. They are now available all year round for, although autumn-flowering, they respond well to artificial day-length and to dwarfing hormones. Place them in good light. Water the pots only when the surface feels dry, then allow them to drain thoroughly before replacing in their covers.

Poinsettias *(Euphorbia pulcherimma),* although forming tall rounded shrubs in their native Mexico, are grown as medium-sized pot plants by nurserymen. The upright stems support star-like bracts which surround the small yellow flowers. These bracts — really modified leaves, are brilliant red in wild plants but may now be obtained in white or pink. Provide a well lit position to produce the best colour in the inflorescence and keep the compost moist without stagnation.

Cissus (Vitidaceae)

This very large genus, closely related to the true vines, *Vitis*, and formerly included with them, contains plants of widely different appearance. Some are succulent and frequently the mature specimens develop massive swollen trunks. This group, when cultivated, is treated in roughly the same way as cactus. Others are fast-growing climbers, well-loved as indoor plants, the evergreens especially, because their leaves have a particularly fresh, clean-cut appearance all year round. The flowers of the various species are insignificant. The name *Cissus* is derived from the Greek name for ivy, *kissos*, no doubt because both have similar clinging stems.

Description *C.antarctica* (Kangaroo vine) is a popular species, originally from Australia. It develops spreading stems which bear short hairy branchlets with shining green, toothed, oval leaves, each with distinctly depressed veins. *C.discolor** is a climber from tropical South-East Asia with remarkably beautifully patterned, green and silver 'quilted' leaves. These have a purple reverse, the whole leaf seemingly made of soft velvet material. This species requires year round high temperature to grow well. *C.rhombifolia* (syn. *Vitis* or *Rhoicissus rhomboidea*, Grape ivy) is a slender-stemmed, evergreen climber which grows wild in the West Indies and Central America. Its young stems and unfurling early leaves are covered in fine white hairs. These leaves are divided into three ovate leaflets, each rhomboid in outline — that is to say with two equal sides and a wedge-shaped base. Each leaflet also has sunken veins and the margins are wavy-toothed. The older stems are brown and hairy and, with the lustrous green of the leaves, make a most attractive combination. The stems may be trained up canes or trellis as they climb readily by means of their coiled tendrils. *Parthenocissus henryi* is one of a group of 15 species from China, closely related to the above and needing similar treatment indoors. The main difference is that these plants are deciduous, or leaf-losing, whereas the others are evergreen. *P.henryi* is, however, greatly valued for its ability to grow well in dark shady places. Training is easy, for its tendrils have adhesive disc-like tips. The thin stems are angled, the leaves divided into five leaflets. These are unequal in size as well as being tapered at each end. The leaves are most pleasing, with the restrained dull olive background highlighting the lacework of silver veins. The best colour develops in the shade. Cut straggling stems back in early spring.

Cultivation These vines require part shade, moderate humidity and a minimum temperature of 5-10°C (41-50°F). Water freely during hot weather and at other times keep the compost just moist. The leaves will greatly benefit from frequent overhead mistings in dry air conditions but must be dry when it is cool or damp. Too much water at these times means a leafless and possibly dead plant. Feed monthly from spring to autumn, using dilute liquid manure. Established plants can be fed with long-term time-release granules. All grow well in a free-draining loam-less mix. Propagate from short stem cuttings rooted in sand. Young shoots with a small piece of old stem usually root best when taken off in spring.

Codiaeum (Euphorbiaceae) Croton

Of this group of evergreen shrubs only one species is in general cultivation and that is represented by a natural variety, *C.variegatum* var. *pictum**.

Description One must not assume from the above statement that the choice is limited, for few plants are so striking or exhibit such diversity of colour and form. Crotons are known for their brilliant leaves in shades of yellow, pink, green, orange and purple, often in riotous mixture on the same plant. It is not simply the leaf colour which varies but also the shape, for some are long ovate and others lobed, resembling the leaves of an oak; then there are kinds reduced in width to become narrow linear. Literally dozens of named sorts of these colourful shrubs have been introduced to the gardening public over the years. Many of these exist now only as names in old books and catalogues. The pale cream-coloured flowers carried in slender spikes are also an attraction as they develop from the upper leaf axils. The male flowers bear five tiny petals which are absent in those of the female.

Cultivation These are basically bushy upright shrubs, the glossy evergreen leaves developing their best colour when exposed to fairly bright indirect light. An average temperature of 16°C (61°F) is needed. As one would imagine with plants originating in Malaysia and the Pacific Islands, they are easiest to manage under conditions of even warmth, together with fairly high humidity, conditions which are not always easily met in the normal home environment. Fortunately they will acclimatise themselves if the original purchase is made in warm weather. They may show their displeasure by shedding a leaf or two on being removed from their ideal surroundings but more should emerge reasonably soon to make good the loss. Plenty of water can be given to the plants when they are growing freely, e.g. in a conservatory or garden room; in the home, the waterings have to be balanced carefully according to the prevailing situation. It is better to allow the compost to drain through between each watering, compensating for the lack of moisture in the pot by freely syringing the leaves with rain water (normal tap water frequently contains lime or other materials which cause unsightly deposits on the smooth leaves). The plants respond well to regular monthly feeding. Once again, balance this to suit the prevailing temperature.

The ideal growing medium for Crotons should be an 'open' mixture to promote aeration and free drainage. Use turfy loam, well broken but not seived, unless to remove the stones, peat and sharp sand. Dry fertilisers can be added at the rate of 2 tablespoons per bucket of mix. Cuttings of half-ripe shoots root readily in a heated propagator. As indoor plants, many specimens eventually become 'leggy' after losing their lower leaves. Try planting some younger plants around them in a large tub to form a superb display. Although some individuals will break naturally into several stems, others are reluctant to do so. Encourage them by pinching out the growing points on two or three occasions.

Coleus (Labiatae) Painted nettle

From this large genus of approximately 150 species one in particular, *C.blumei,* sometimes also called the Flame nettle* in its developed forms, both seedlings and named cultivar, is valued as an indoor plant. It is fascinating to read old books and nursery catalogues where many individually named sorts are listed. Although plants are available in a host of superb leaf colour combinations, today these are invariably derived from seed-raised plants. The best are sometimes perpetuated by rooting cuttings as were the old-time sorts. They are, in fact, perennials but, as their display life tends to be limited in an indoor situation, most growers consider them as plants of annual duration only.

Description *C.blumei* is an upright branching plant with square rather fleshy green stems, sometimes streaked with purple or dark green markings. The typical nettle-like leaves which are the plant's special feature were pointed ovate in shape in the original introductions from Java, where they are still found growing wild. In today's cultivated kinds, we have plants with leaves of various forms. The margins are invariably deeply toothed although occasionally they may be scalloped. The leaf colour could be said to range from quietly attractive through sumptuous to bizarre! The quiet shades, such as pale citron, green, white, apricot and pink, all in various combinations, give way to browns, purple and scarlet. It is the latter colours that give the common name, Flame nettle, real meaning. The leaves are patterned in a profusion of different designs, all of which may be maintained by rooting stem cuttings. It is best to remove the spikes, or terminal racemes, of small blue flowers as they appear; this will result in a more compact leafy specimen. Use these relatively easy-to-grow plants individually or massed in a planter. Do not, however, overcrowd the pots because they require freely circulating air at all times.

Cultivation Sun or part shade suits these plants and a minimum temperature of 7°C (44.5°F) is required. The finest plants develop where the air is moving yet warm and humid. Ample water may be given to established plants from spring through summer, together with a dilute liquid feed once each week. During cooler weather, particularly when they are semi-dormant, the watering should be decreased, so that the compost may drain through and become almost dry. Loam-less compost is suitable for potting, as is sandy loam. Propagation is easy, either from seed or from summer-rooted tip cuttings.

Clerodendron (Verbenaceae)

Clerodendron numbers well over 300 species and is widely distributed in tropical regions, particularly in Africa and Malaysia. The name comes from *kleros* (=chance) and *dendron* (=tree), probably because of the medicinal properties of various species. They are either climbing plants or shrubs. They are renowned for their brilliant displays in glass-houses and conservatories. *C.speciosissimum* (Glory bush) Java is especially magnificent when carrying its large terminal panicles of brilliant orange-red flowers.

Description *C.thomsonae* (Glory bower, Bleeding heart vine)* develops climbing stems clad with opposite pairs of thin, dark green, pointed ovate leaves. The small brilliant crimson-red flowers contrast remarkably with the stark greeny-white of their calices.

Cultivation *Clerodendron* are best in diffused sunlight or semi-shade, minimum temperature 12°C (53.5°F). Water freely when making new growth; less at other times. Light liquid feeding encourages the production of new wood which, in turn, should mean more flowers, although the species described is remarkably unreliable in this respect. For potting, use a mixture of leaf mould, loam and sand. Increase is by cuttings of the current season's wood in early summer.

Coffea (Rubiaceae)

This genus of some 40 shrubs and small trees is found in tropical Asia and Africa. The name comes from the Arabic word for coffee which is produced commercially from several species. *C.arabica* provides high quality 'beans' when young and is a useful indoor plant.

Description *C.arabica* (Arabian coffee tree)* is a much branched, eventually large, evergreen shrub which, under ideal growing conditions, attains as much as 4 m (13ft) in height. Naturally, this will be considerably less indoors. The leaves are thin and wavy-edged, carried in opposite pairs, elliptic in outline, tapering to a slender point, dark glossy green above and paler beneath. The fragrant white flowers, produced in clusters of four or five from the upper leaf axils, and followed by bright red, fleshy berries, each containing two seeds are unfortunately seldom seen in the home. Use them individually.

Cultivation These require constant warm humid conditions with bright, filtered light, minimum temperature 16°C (61°F). Ample water can be given, but the pots must on no account become waterlogged. Feed by sprinkling slow-release fertiliser granules over the pot surface or top-dress with fertilised compost during the early part of the season. When re-potting use a mixture of sandy loam and peat. Propagate from cuttings of half-ripe wood.

59

Columnea (Gesneriaceae) Goldfish plants

The indoor plants from this group were selected from a large genus of tropical American sub-shrubs and epiphytes. Room plants are almost always epiphytes. Their name was given in honour of the author Fabius Columna (1567–1640), who wrote *Phytobasanos,* the earliest botanical work to include copper plates.

Description Some *Columnea* are bushy, others trailing, and there are intermediates between these two typical forms. Those which trail include some remarkable plants with completely pendulous growth. All are evergreen with their opposite, dark green leaves either hairy or densely covered in fine down. The bright showy flowers are tubular in shape with an extended hood-like upper lip. The lower lip is parted into three spreading segments. The flowers, which appear in winter and spring, and intermittently at other times, are produced from the upper leaf axils and are clustered or solitary, according to the species. *C.allenii* is a slender-stemmed trailer from Panama with pairs of dark green leaves and large hooded orange-red blooms. *C.arguta,* also from Panama and a trailer, has stems clad with small, pointed, ovate leaves and comparatively large salmon-red flowers. *C.* × *banksii* is a splendid sight in spring when the arching stems, with pairs of bristly leaves, are covered along their length with bright orange flowers. *C.gloriosa** is a Costa Rican native with strictly pendant shoots, densely and regularly clothed with soft, purplish leaves. The hooded flowers are rich red, with the open blooms displaying a yellow throat. *C.microphylla* is similar but smaller, particularly its leaves which are rounded in shape. The large flowers are coppery-red with wide open petals. *C.* × *'Stavanger'* (Norse fire plant) is a fine hybrid, raised in Norway, with spreading stems; the glossy green leaves are spaced out and the flowers are orange and red. All of the *Columnea* mentioned above may be grown in hanging baskets, an essential treatment for the kinds with branches which hang straight down. Those with arching stems may be potted for placing on a shelf or wall bracket.

Cultivation These plants require a warm, lightly shaded position with a high temperature throughout the year, minimum 15°C (59°F). Lower temperature is acceptable for 4 to 6 weeks prior to flowering, provided that the plants are completely dormant and kept almost dry. At all other times, the humidity should be maintained at a high level. Keep your plants moist when they are growing, reducing water in late autumn to induce a winter rest period. If time-release granules are used for feeding, little else is needed. Should additional feeding be necessary use a natural organic material, e.g. dried blood, well diluted, at 2-monthly intervals. The potting soil must be rich in humus. Equal parts of rotted leaf mould and peat, plus a little crushed charcoal, is suggested as a good growing medium. Propagate by rooting short stem cuttings in moist sandy compost. After watering allow the leaves to dry off before covering the pot with a plastic bag. Left too wet there is real danger of rot setting in before the cuttings have time to root.

Cordyline (Agavaceae)

This small group, some of which are eventually large-growers, comes from several countries which border the Pacific and Indian Oceans. While they remain small, many make useful patio and indoor plants of tropical appearance.

Description Members of the genus *Cordyline* are evergreen with the leaves often long and narrow. Frequently these are tough and leathery too. They at first radiate from a single stout stem which later in life may elongate to form a trunk. In other smaller-growers several stems topped with clustered leaves are more usual. The often large panicles of white or lilac, sweetly scented flowers are seldom seen when the plants are in the confines of a small pot. *C.australis* (Cabbage tree or Grass palm) is an eventually tall plant attaining 10 m (33 ft) plus in the wild. They remain small enough, however, to make them of value for many seasons when grown inside. The single trunk is crowned by a fountain of long narrow, green or bronze leaves. *C.indivisa* (Mountain cabbage tree) is a New Zealand wild plant, its broad leaves clearly marked with a red mid-rib. Water it often. *C.terminalis* (Tree of kings) has produced, in its several colourful cultivars, a selection of plants with their leaves marked in a range of flamboyant pinks, yellows and reds. Such a plant is *C.* 'Celestial Dawn'* which, at the time of writing, is being developed as an international indoor plant. This is a particularly desirable acquisition, thriving in warm humid conditions.

Cultivation The larger-growers — *C.australis* especially, make fine patio plants for the summer months. They need ample moisture at this time and good light but prefer to be out of the blistering heat of the sun. Remember that these plants are only hardy in mild districts. Indoors they should be fairly dry during the winter with a minimum temperature of 7°C (44.5°F). Smaller-growers, which include any with brightly coloured leaves, need more sheltered warmer places to develop and must be kept inside the year round, minimum temperature 15°C (59°F). These need good light and humidity with some movement of air. All *Cordyline* appreciate plenty of water during hot weather but, when it becomes cool, reduce the frequency of watering so that the compost becomes partially dry each time. When re-potting is needed, include loam in the mixture, if making it up yourself, and peat and sharp sand in the proportion of 7 to 3 to 1. The New Zealand species can be increased by sowing their seeds in light compost. The other kinds, which seem to get confused with *Dracaena*, may have unwanted sideshoots rooted as cuttings. Reduce the leaf area by trimming them back before inserting these in a heated frame. Fine new plants of this group can also be procured by wounding the stem just below the crown of leaves. This is the mossed by securing moist sphagnum moss around the stem with black plastic film. When new roots are observed bursting through the base of the 'package', it may be severed and the new plant potted up.

Ctenanthe (Marantaceae)

The name of this genus, a small one of 15 species, was developed from the Greek, *kteis* (=comb) and *anthos* (=flower). This refers to the comb-like arrangement of the flower bracts.

Description The individual members of the genus *Maranta* are natives of Brazil. They are similar in general appearance, with long-stalked basal leaves, oval in shape. As the plant grows, it develops a branching structure of slender stems. *C.lubbersiana**, named in honour of C.Lubbers (1832–1905), who was, during his lifetime, the head gardener at the Botanic Garden, Brussels, Belgium, has dark green leaves, heavily striped with white and yellow variegations. *C.oppenheimiana* is a free-growing species, particularly when removed from the restrictions of a pot. Its leaves are dark grey-green with silver-grey bands between the veins and wine-red beneath. *C.o.* 'Tricolor' is a lovely plant to own, more compact than its original form with rather narrow leaves well marked with grey, cream and white with occasional red lines. Curled leaf edges turn back to reveal the rich red coloration of the under surface.

With their colourful leaves, use *Ctenanthe* to provide a tropical appearance in indoor gardens or planters. Placed individually, the open leaf arrangement of a plant can be particularly useful to the home decorator as it makes a dramatic display against a plain wall.

Cultivation These tropical plants luxuriate in warmth and shade the year round. An ideal minimum temperature of 15°C (59°F) should be the aim, although these plants will tolerate cooler conditions if their compost is fairly dry at the time. As is the case with almost all other plants of tropical origin, the watering has to be carefully regulated according to the temperature, at all times high humidity being preferable to 'wet feet'. With *Ctanthe,* even when the plants are growing well, it is better for them to be partially dry between each application of water. Gentle feeding may be applied. The young plants in particular respond well to an organic-based liquid fertiliser. Use this at monthly intervals during the spring and summer. A sprinkling of time-release granules will provide sufficent nourishment for older, established plants. Loam-based compost suits these best. Use a standard mixture of 3 parts sterilised loam, 2 parts peat, 1 part sharp sand. Proportions for this compost are by bulk and not weight and of course this will need the addition of fertilisers to provide nourishment. Stock increase is by rooting cuttings of the stems taken off complete with a leaf. Insert these in a warm frame during the summer months. Alternatively, divide up an old plant when it is dormant.

Cuphea (Lythraceae)

Description *C.hyssopifolia* (False heather) is a wiry-stemmed shrublet whose delicate appearance belies its toughness. It has tiny, leathery, dark green leaves, linear in shape, and small purple-pink flowers, each held in a green calyx and displayed profusely for many weeks from early spring on. *C.platycentra* (syn. *C.ignea,* Cigar flower)* is a small evergreen shrub with opposite lanceolate leaves, introduced from Mexico in 1848. The drooping flowers, freely produced, have a calyx only; the orange-red tube displays a white interior rimmed with dark red and black.

Cultivation These plants are useful for a sunny window-sill where temperatures never fall below 10°C (50°F). When frosts are likely, move them into a warm part of the room, although thick curtains can also insulate them. Free amounts of water can be given when they are in active growth; less in dull weather. Their compost must not be allowed to dry out, even in cold weather. Apply liquid feed monthly while the plants are in flower. Any free-draining compost is suitable, preferably reasonably rich, containing some hoof and horn fertiliser. After potting up, the shoots can be pinched back on two or three occasions to promote dense, dwarf growth. The little bushes can be trimmed back during the winter to prevent them from becoming straggly. Propagate by half-ripe cuttings or seeds. The latter flower early in life.

Cyanotis (Commelinaceae)

Very few of this genus from Somaliland are cultivated indoors. Their name comes from *kyanos* (=blue) and *ous*, (=ear), which refer to the ear-like petals of the flowers.

Description *C.somaliensis* (Pussy ears)* is a pretty plant covered in long white silky hairs with well branched fleshy stems bearing narrow, shiny, olive-green leaves which are sheathing at their base. When individuals of this species are grown 'hard' (potted in poor compost or one deficient in nutrients) and receive a minimal amount of water, the leaves are smaller and more triangular in outline and the plant extremely dense and rounded. The tiny, bright blue flowers typically bear three petals and are displayed over several weeks in spring. Grow for individual display on window-sills or in hanging baskets.

Cultivation These plants require a sunny or well lit position, minimum temperature 10°C (50°C). The pots may be allowed to become virtually dry between each heavy watering. Although primarily foliage plants, a spartan diet will result in more flowers. Re-potting compost can consist of loam and leaf mould or peat in equal parts plus enough sand to ensure sharp drainage. Slightly fertilised loam-less mix is also satisfactory. Increasing plants from small tip cuttings is relatively easy but remember not to apply any water from overhead until they are well rooted and potted on.

Cycas (Cycadaceae) Sago palm

These plants, of extreme interest to the botanist for their flowering characteristics and method of growth, were once, like the tree ferns and many conifers, much more widespread over the globe. The Sago palms are so named on account of a coarse type of sago obtained from some kinds which are tropical in origin. Most species are suited for hot-house cultivation only. We find that one species, *C.revoluta*, is becoming increasingly used as an indoor plant, and successfully too.

Description *C.revoluta* (Sago palm)*, which is sometimes seen sporting the label *C.inermis*, forms a rosette of arching fern-like leaves, small when young then developing into fronds of great length and becoming more palm-like when older. When the plant is immature, these leaves develop from what is in effect a large bud at ground level, the stem gradually elongating with age into a stout cylindrical trunk, 1-3 m (3¼-9¾ft) in height, the whole plant then being of particularly bold and handsome appearance. The tough, leathery leaves are pinnate, i.e. feather-like, arranged in two ranks or rows, dark green above and paler beneath, with rolled edges which become brown spines at their tips. This species is a native of Japan, China and parts of the East Indies. Although eventually very tall, with an immense head of leaves, this kind of *Cycas* will tolerate the confines of a moderately-sized pot for a number of years before requiring a greater amount of space. Indeed they may be planted out into a sheltered spot in the garden in those countries where only light frosts occur. Elsewhere they are frequently placed outside during the summer months to provide a tropical effect on a patio.

Cultivation Place the pots of *Cycas* in light shade, minimum temperature 10°C (50°F). Water the plants freely in warm weather but less when cool or damp. Little in the way of regular liquid feeding is needed by the larger of the indoor plants as there should be sufficient nutrient incorporated in the compost. When this is exhausted, time-release capsules can be used to continue the feeding. For the young plants, an occasional watering with an organic fertiliser, such as dried blood, will be to their advantage. Make this up into a liquid and apply it to the pots after they have been well saturated with water; then arrange for the interval before the plant gets its next watering to be as long as possible in order for the fertiliser to do its work. The compost used for re-potting can comprise either a standard loam-less mix, in which case feeding with a side-dressing will be needed during the first and subsequent seasons of growth, or a well drained mixture of loam and sand with a proportion of added peat. The propagation of Sago palms is from imported seeds which are obtained from the countries of origin. Here they develop within the large cone-like former inflorescence. The seeds are normally only available in trade quantities and are individually fairly expensive.

Cyclamen (Primulaceae) Florist cyclamen

C.persicum, found wild from Greece to Syria and one of 16 species in the genus, is the ancestor of all the modern kinds we know. These are extremely popular as colourful, indoor, flowering pot plants. Their name comes from *kyclos* (=circular), either because they all have round corms (tubers) or because, in many kinds, there is a tight spiralling of the elongated stalk after flowering — a peculiarity incidentally not seen in *C.persicum.*

Description The wild plant is small-growing and very dainty, with scented flowers — an attribute unfortunately lost in the majority of the present day descendants. Growth is from a flattened, hard, round tuber covered in corky skin and rooting only from below (be warned about this for re-potting). From this tuber arise, during late summer, fleshy-stemmed heart-shaped leaves which are dark green, mottled or zoned in silver-grey. These develop into a tufted rosette. The solitary flowers are likewise produced on fleshy stems with their pointed buds at first curving downwards. Soon these unfurl to display the large nodding swan-like flowers. There are today several strains with single* or double blooms, some with frilled petals. The colours include white, pink, red and maroon.

Such colourful plants have a wide variety of uses in the home — to add interest to an indoor garden, as individual specimens or to fill a planter. As an 'accent plant' placed on a low table in the lounge, they are ideal and, as they may be had in bloom from the festive season to Mother's Day, they are favourite gifts in the northern hemisphere.

Cultivation For the best results, with a long season of flowering, a light position with cool moist air should be selected. If the plants are used to decorate a warm lounge, remove them to a cooler place as often as possible. *Cyclamen* flower to perfection in a 10-18°C (50-64.5°F) temperature range. Water the pots from the base, both when the plants are developing and when they are flowering, allowing the compost to become partly dry each time. Liquid feeding can be undertaken every 2 weeks, even when flowering has ceased. When most of the leaves have wilted or yellowed, watering may be halted. Now is the time to stand the pots outside in the sun until the soil is completely dry. After a rest of several weeks, the plants need re-potting. To do this, twist the tuber into the surface of a filled pot so that it is scarcely half-embedded. Use a standard potting soil mix or one composed of 1 part each of loam, leaf mould and sand plus fertilisers. Also add ground limestone (chalk) at the rate of 1 tablespoon per bucket of mixed compost. *Cyclamen* are propagated by sowing seeds during the spring or summer. Space these out at equal distance for even growth. Grow them on, re-potting as required in a draught-free even temperature.

Dieffenbachia (Araceae) Dumb cane

This is a genus of some 20 or more species from tropical South America, much valued on account of their handsome evergreen foliage which is frequently, in the cultivated kinds, superbly marked in a contrasting colour. Herr Dieffenbach, after whom the genus is named, was a gardener at Schonbrunn, Austria, during 1830. Their common name derives from the fact that the sap contained in the stems and leaves is extremely acrid. It is said to cause intense pain should it come into contact with unprotected eyes, mouth or throat. The tissues swell, resulting in loss of speech. Workers on nurseries where these plants are propagated are warned of the dangers and told not to eat or smoke after handling the plants. However, we personally know of no adults who, except for allergic conditions, have been affected in any way when dealing with poisonous plants. On the other hand we do know people whose health has suffered damage due to long-term careless exposure to chemicals used in horticulture.

Description *Dieffenbachia* have rather fleshy upright stems bearing stalked, smooth, mostly ovate leaves with prominent mid-rib and veins. The flowers, which are not always seen in an indoor situation, are small, pale green or white, and arum-like. *D. picta* (Spotted dumb cane)* and its many cultivars, each with a distinctive feature, are the more frequently seen of the genus. The leaves of these vary from some with creamy-white variegations, which contrast remarkably well with the dark green of the background, to others, such as *D.p.* 'Rudolph Roehrs', in which the two leaf colours are separate and yellow-white extends over almost the whole leaf.

Use these favourite decorator plants singly as bold specimens or to provide good height in a mixed arrangement.

Cultivation Dumb canes make a valuable contribution to the range of lovely things we can grow indoors. Although shade is tolerated, to promote the best leaf coloration, the plants should be sited where they receive the maximum amount of indirect light. They require year round warmth — minimum temperature 12°C (53.5°F), no draughts or fumes from fires and regular overhead syringing in hot dry weather. Their water supply has to be watched carefully, for the roots rot off rather easily under cool air conditions. It is advisable to let the pots get dry almost to the point of the leaves wilting before giving them a thorough soak, using tepid water. When making up your own compost for these plants, use equal parts of turfy loam, peat or leaf mould, and well rotted manure (or double amount of leaf mould) together with some sharp sand. The pots must be well drained to promote the quickest possible run-through of water. Suckers, which develop from the base of the older plants, can be used for increase. A cutting comprising a piece of stem complete with leaf will also root under the correct conditions of warmth and humidity.

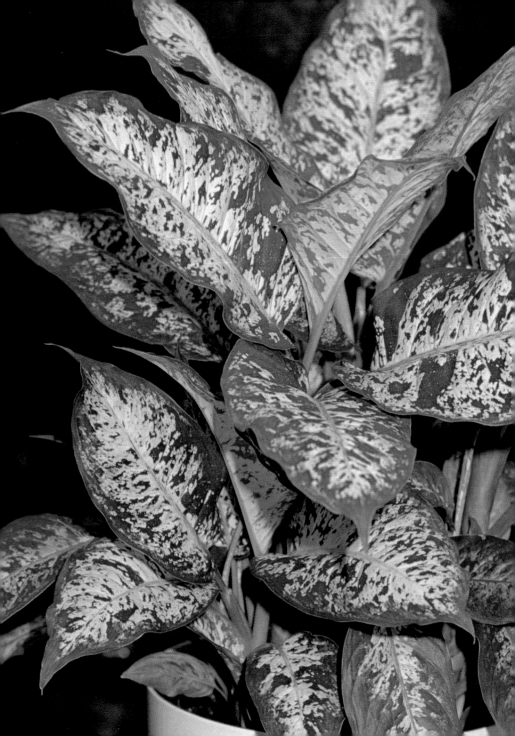

Dizygotheca (Araliaceae)

This is a genus of 17 members, all shrubs and small trees native to Australia and islands of the Pacific. The strange-sounding name is made up of three words and refers to the twice normal number of cells in the anthers; hence *di* (= two), *zygos* (=yoke), *theka* (= case).

Description   *D. elegantissima** the only species likely to be encountered growing as a house plant, was introduced into cultivation from the New Hebrides in 1873. It is an upright grower, thinly branched with each long-stalked, palmate leaf composed of indented segments. The leaves, which are a rich metallic bronze in colour, as well as the overall dainty appearance of the young plants, immediately endears these to the floral decorator, who knows that gold or yellow flowers go perfectly with the bronze leaves when the two are placed together in a mixed planter. Also the delicate form of the False aralia, as it is sometimes called, can be as valuable to them as a rare work of art, particularly if placed where shadows are cast upon a wall.

Cultivation   To grow this plant to perfection it must be in a shady spot, minimum temperature 15°C (59°F). Humidity should also be high, which entails frequent misting over during dry weather. When watering, keep the pots just evenly moist during the winter, allowing the plants a little more water when the weather becomes warmer. Frequent liquid feeding at monthly intervals, when all other requirements are met, will result in well-grown bushy, upright plants. The normal method of increase is from seeds. These are not produced by the plants we grow indoors so may not be available, except in commercial quantities. Air-layering or 'mossing' is consequently the method of increase best suited to the home gardener.

Note: As with other plants and shrubs of similar tropical zone origins, *Dizygotheca* will tolerate, for short periods, temperatures lower than the minimum quoted. There are several factors involved here, including the age of the individual and whether their stems are well-ripened, with the compost rather drier than they would otherwise enjoy. Should the plants become accidently frosted under these conditions, they must on no account be brought directly into a heated room or they will have only a remote chance of survival. If, however, they are first of all put into a cool, shaded place, misted over with water and then gradually returned to warmer conditions after several days, their chances of living are greatly enhanced. However, even then, the extent of the permanent damage will not become apparent for some time.

Dracaena (Agavaceae) Dragon lily

These favourite indoor plants are natives of the tropics where they range in size from upright shrubs to small trees. They are cultivated for their evergreen leaves, which are frequently boldly striped or mottled in a contrasting colour.

Description   When they are young, the leaves of *Dracaena* are ribbon-like and arranged in the form of a tuft or rosette. As the plants age, their stems elongate to become a short, sometimes fairly thick, trunk. *D.deremensis* (Striped dracaena) comes from tropical Africa. In the cultivar *D.d.* 'Warneckii' we have a tall plant with narrow leaves, each marked with longitudinal bands of white. *D.fragrans* 'Massangeana'* is a sturdy-grower with broad, arching, dark green leaves striped with yellow-gold. *D. godseffiana* (Gold dust dracaena) is a smaller-growing sort, with deep, glossy green leaves finely speckled in yellow. As the leaves age these spots become white. *D.marginata* 'Tricolor' (Rainbow tree) is an upright species and, when it is grown in bright light, the narrow arching leaves display a green centre bordered on each side with cream; this in turn is heavily suffused with a bright pinkish-red which extends to the leaf edges. It is an altogether lovely plant, with its fountain of colourful leaves rivalling anything else we grow indoors. *D.sanderiana,* from the Congo, is a small neat-grower, normally developing as a plant with several tufts of narrow, white-margined, deep green leaves.

All of these species are much valued indoors, either when used individually or as foliage contrast in a mixed arrangement.

Cultivation   Diffuse to fairly bright light is required to bring out the best leaf colour of *Dracaena* and a minimum temperature of 15°C (59°F). A higher temperature with good humidity is needed for these plants to really flourish yet, as mentioned for *Dizygotheca,* many tropical plants are able to withstand cooler conditions if they are resting from active growth and in fairly dry compost. Their normal cultivation requirement is for plenty of water and moist compost at all times. This does not, of course, mean that they can stand in water. They also appreciate being misted overhead frequently in hot weather, but not when a cool period is likely to follow. Should your plant develop brown spots on the leaves, water lodging there overnight may well be the cause. A compost as suggested for *Cordyline,* to which genus these are closely related, can be used for re-potting. At the time of writing we have beside the desk a fine Rainbow tree which is growing well in a 50/50 mixture of peat and fine sand. This receives a thorough drench with organic liquid fertiliser every fourth week right through the growing season, which for us is most of the year. The tops of old overgrown plants can be rooted. After severing, strip away some of the lower leaves by pulling them downwards in order to expose a short piece of stem. Put the stems into sandy compost and place the pots in a warm place for roots to form.

Epiphyllum (Cactaceae) Orchid cactus

The Latin name for this group of colourful cacti was derived from the two words *epi* (=on) and *phyllon* (=leaf), because the flowers appear to spring from the edges of the 'leaves', which are really phyllodes (Bot. a leaf-like stem). There are about 16 species in the genus, all natives of tropical America and occur from Mexico to Brazil. They are mostly epiphytic in the wild, either attached to trees, where their roots penetrate the debris which has gathered in the forks of the branches, or on mounds of fallen litter at the base of the trunk.

Description All *Epiphyllum* are characterised by their leathery, flattened leaf/stems which are sometimes three-angled at the base. Most of these leaves have crenate margins, i.e. the edges are bluntly toothed. Stiff hairs grow out of these indentations. Real spines, almost the hallmark of the cactus family, are absent or only noticed on small seedlings. The specimens used to decorate our homes are virtually all hybrid in origin and are crosses not only between the various *Epiphyllum* species but also between *Epiphyllum* and other closely related genera. The results are sometimes called *E.ackermannii*, after an early hybrid. *E.* × *hybridum* is to be preferred. The named kinds are said to number over 1,000 and are floriferous with spectacular funnel-shaped blooms in a wide range of colours*.

Cultivation Always remember their forest beginnings when siting these plants in the home. Select an airy place in the light shade for the best results, minimum temperature 10°C (50°F). Water frequently in warm weather, and mist over unopened flower buds. Later, when the annual growth has ceased, watering should be less frequent to allow the pots to become partially dry each time. Liquid feed can be applied once each month from before to well after flowering has ceased. In addition to needing more water than their desert-dwelling cactus relatives, *Epiphyllum* prefer a humus-rich compost rather than a spartan diet. This may be peat alone, with added fertiliser and frequent liquid feeding, or a mixture of peat and leaf mould with sand added for drainage. Propagate your special plants from firm stem cuttings. Sowing seed will result in a good mixture of colours, not necessarily the same as the seed-parent.

Episcia (Gesneriaceae)

The botanical name of these charming small evergreen plants comes from the Greek *episkios* (=shaded), probably because of their South American rain forest origins.

Description *Episcia* are invariably low-growing or creeping plants; their leaves are an added attraction to the pretty tubular or open bell-shaped flowers. *E.cupreata* (Flame violet) is the parent of several named cultivars. *E.c.* 'Acajou'* is actually a hybrid. Its leaves are basically deep brown but with areas of metallic silver and silver veins. The blooms are rich orange. *E. c.* 'Chocolate Soldier' is another fine example with chocolate-brown leaves making a foil for the orange-scarlet flowers. Ideally these are warm greenhouse plants, needing a draught-free constant warmth with high humidity. Surprisingly enough they will also grow well in a normal living room, if planted in a basket and placed in a window.

Cultivation Put your *Episcia* in a well lit spot out of the direct rays of the sun, minimum temperature 15°C (59°F). Keep the roots just moist throughout the year, being careful not to splash the foliage when watering. Potting compost can be made up using the various humus materials available or use a proprietary African violet mixture. To increase your plants, try dividing the rooting stems. A knife cut may be needed to sever the shoots. Do this with care and gently tease the roots apart.

Euphorbia (Euphorbiaceae) Spurge

Containing over 2,000 species, this genus is remarkable both for its size and its diversity: weedy annuals, attractive herbaceous plants, shrubs bearing normal leaves and succulents, tiny and great, with leaves frequently reduced to sharp spines. They are distributed worldwide, with Africa being the headquarters of the succulent group. To confirm the identity of a *Euphorbia,* cut the stem; a milky latex will be exuded.

Description   *E.milii splendens* (syn. *E.splendens prostrata,* Crown of thorns)* is a virtually prostrate shrub with irregular-branched stems, cylindrical, succulent and greyish in colour and heavily armed with long tapering spines. The bright green leaves are lanceolate, sparse and chiefly clustered at the tips of the branches. The flowers on this showy species from Malagasy appear in spring and are held in cymes or clusters, each on a short red peduncle(stem); they consist of two bright red, rounded bracts.

Cultivation   Put these in good light — a sunny window-sill is ideal, minimum temperature 10°C (50°F). Water the plants often when in flower — less at other times, keeping them almost dry during their winter rest period. For potting, use a mixture of well drained loam to which some fine bone meal has been added. Increase your stock from stem cuttings in which the cut surface is allowed to air-dry before insertion into moist sand.

Fatsia (Araliaceae) Japanese aralia

Reasonably frost-hardy, *F.japonica* is an easily grown, decorative evergreen with large, glossy green leaves. Although it eventually develops into a fairly large specimen it is particularly suited to cool, shaded rooms in the home.

Description   The stalked leaves which grow from thick grey shoots are broadly palmate in *F.japonica*, i.e. hand-like with the lobes of the leaf representing fingers. These lobes are toothed, wavy-edged and pointed. The large branching panicles of starry flowers which are carried on established plants are milk-white in colour. They are later followed by round black berries. These are not always seen indoors, which is unfortunate, for both flowers and fruit contrast delightfully with the plants' polished dark green leaves. *F.japonica* (syn. *Aralia sieboldii*)* was introduced, in 1838, into western cultivation from Japan where it is a native. It was immediately popular with Victorian gardeners in large cities who, among other things, had the problem of smoky deposits on anything they planted out of doors and gas fires to poison plants grown inside. The Japanese aralia survived in both situations and is recently enjoying a return to popularity.

Use small specimens in hangers; larger plants can be accommodated in a shady corner. Even old individuals, which have lost many of their lower leaves, are still an attraction with their grey, trunk-like stems topped with shiny, dark green foliage of a decidedly tropical appearance.

Cultivation   Select a cool shady spot for these foliage plants. Since they are hardy over most of the temperate regions they will tolerate temperatures as low as 5°C (41°F). They require sufficient water to maintain the compost in a just moist condition through the year. Feed the plant monthly with dilute liquid fertiliser during the spring and summer. *Fatsia* are easily grown in most soils whether containing loam or not. Their leaves require regular cleaning to keep them looking fresh and a watch should be kept for brown scale insect which is a pest of these plants. Seed, if it is available, is the best way of raising new plants. It germinates readily and, before long, the seedlings will be large enough to be potted up and used for display. Offsets or suckers sometimes appear on older plants. These may be detached and grown on. Old stems can also be air-layered by mossing just below the crowns of leaves.

× Fatshedera (Araliaceae) Ivy tree

Raised in France in 1910, × *Fatshedera lizei** was the result of a remarkable marriage when *Fatsia japonica moseri* was pollinated by *Hedera helix* 'Hibernica' (Irish ivy).

Description   Grown indoors, it first forms an upright bush then, if left, tends to sprawl. The plants therefore must be pruned back fairly hard each spring or trained up canes or trellis. The latter method is to be preferred. In the original plant, the leaves are leathery, deeply five-lobed and dark lustrous green in colour. In × *F.l.* 'Variegata', each leaf edge is prettily margined in cream. These are both tough plants, ideally suited to difficult situations — even low light areas. To a certain extent both draughts and fumes are also coped with.

Cultivation   Grow these plants in a shady spot, temperature 6°C (42.5°F). Water the pots freely when new growth is being made; allow them to partially dry between each watering at other times. Feed monthly with liquid fertiliser to encourage plentiful fine foliage during the spring and summer. Due to their manner of growth, which can become top-heavy, Ivy trees are sometimes regarded as short-term room plants. Cuttings of the upright shoots root readily during the spring. Three of these placed in a pot will quickly form an attractive plant. Red spider mite can be troublesome under dry air conditions. Frequent overhead mistings using plain water will discourage these unwelcome pests.

Fittonia (Acanthaceae)

This is a genus of two evergreen herbaceous plants, originally discovered in Peru. Their flowers, held in a terminal bract, are undistinguished and, when produced, may be removed. It is for the beautifully marked leaves that these plants are grown.

Description   *F.verschaffeltii* (Mosaic plant) has dark green leaves marked with bright red veins. Of its two natural variants, *F.v.argyroneura* (Nerve plant)* has light green leaves, densely patterned with a tracery of white veins. *F.v.pearcei* (Snake skin plant)* also has pale leaves but with pinkish veins. Culture under warm humid conditions is relatively easy. Small specimens can be planted in a terrarium or glass container; larger pots should be plunged into a peat-filled planter.

Cultivation   High humidity and light shade is required, with a minimum temperature of 15°C (59°F). Keep the pots moist at all times. Frequent overhead misting during hot weather is desirable, for the leaf edges, being thin, dry rather easily. A potting compost of loam, peat and sharp sand, or a standard soil-less mix, give good results. New plants can be raised by means of 'Irishman's' cuttings — another name for partly rooted divisions! Treat these as you would unrooted tips until they are well rooted. Preferably keep them under glass or plastic. Greenfly(aphids) are a particularly troublesome pest if not kept in check.

85

Ficus (Moraceae)

This is a vast genus, containing over 600 species from the tropics or sub-tropics. They range in stature from the tiny creepers or trailers, such as *F.pumila minima,* up to the 30 m (98 ft) height of *F.religiosa,* the sacred Bo tree of India. The delicious fig of commerce is another member of the family. When in their young stage, several *Ficus,* including the universally popular India rubber tree, *F.elastica,* make splendid room plants.

Description   *F.benjamina* (Weeping fig) is a vigorous grower although the growth rate depends ōn various factors, e.g. pot size and situation selected for display. Eventually this will become a medium-sized tree indoors. Its weeping branches hang from an upright trunk and carry pendulous leaves. . These are long ovate, tapering to a slender point and shining green in colour. The young plants of *F.elastica* 'Decora'* are stout-stemmed with what is normally a single, upright trunk holding large, lustrous green, ovate leaves, each ending in a hook-like point. The depressed veins almost at right angles to the ivory-coloured mid-rib render the leaf surface slightly corrugated. Even temperatures with good light will produce stocky specimens with closely set leaves. *F.elastica* 'Doescheri'* has leaves in shades of green, grey-green, yellow and white, frequently with a pink flush. This is a very attractive cultivar with a strikingly different style of leaf variegation. *F.elastica* 'Variegata'* has its rather more narrow, leathery, green leaves edged with clear light yellow; other areas are overlaid with grey-green. *F.lyrata* (Fiddle-leaf fig) bears large, boldly handsome, lustrous green leaves, round-ended and waved, distinctly waisted or fiddle-shaped. This upright grower, of particularly bold appearance, thrives best in a large planter. *F.pumila* (Creeping fig) is a climbing or creeping plant which will cling to walls or other supports much like an ivy but with considerably smaller leaves. These are pale brown at first, then light green, becoming really dark only with age. The tiny leaves have a blistered surface and are oval in outline, each with a heart-shaped base. They may be used either to clothe a shady wall or to fill a basket with a mass of verdure.

Cultivation   Although a generally light shade is preferred, most kinds of *Ficus* are adaptable regarding the amount of light tolerated; minimum temperature is 10–15°C (50–59°F). Moderate amounts of water may be given when temperature, light and humidity are high enough to promote new growth. Keep the pots of the large-growers fairly dry under cool conditions. Regular monthly feeding is advised, particularly if the plants are growing in a soil-less compost. Rubber trees grow well in any free-draining medium, either soil-based or loam-less.Those species with large evergreen leaves require frequent sponging to remove dust which always seems to accumulate remarkably quickly. Most kinds can be increased bẙ rooting tip cuttings in moist sand over bottom heat. Unless a propagator with intermittent mist is being used, it is as well to reduce the transpiration of the large leaves by cutting them in half. This does not spoil the appearance of the plant for, if very short cuttings are utilised, these lower leaves are soon discarded after rooting. Air-layering with a moss 'pillow' is sometimes used both to increase the plant and, at the same time, to reduce the height of an oldish resident of the living room.

Fuchsia (Onagraceae)

This genus is made up of 100 species which are found from Central to South America and in the West Indies, Tahiti and New Zealand.

Description Most *Fuchsia* are shrubs or climbers when seen in the wild. In New Zealand — the home of five species in all, *F.excorticata* grows into a fairly substantial tree with papery scaling bark and *F.procumbens* spreads thin stems along the ground and points its tiny yellow flowers skywards! Such is the diversity of nature. Except for *F.magellanica,* its varieties and cultivars, nearly all of the *Fuchsia* we grow in our gardens are hybrid in origin. Several thousand different ones have been named in the past and these are constantly being added to. As well as being very useful in the garden, they are also outstanding in the glass- or shade-house. As indoor plants they do not rate as highly as they do outdoors, simply because most people who can grow them to perfection elsewhere find that bringing them into the house results in an almost immediate loss of all the flowers. Before very long, the leaves also begin to drop until only a bare framework of branches is left. This is because present day *Fuchsia* are particularly susceptible to abrupt changes in light and humidity. They require a long period in which to acclimatise. If, in fact, they are placed in a light window as young plants, they will not only grow well but should flower profusely. The older small-flowered cultivars, such as 'Alice Hoffman', 'Balkon' and 'Princess Dollar', are more reliable in this respect. Some kinds with pendulous growth are fine when suspended in a moderately well lit window. The cultivar 'Marinka'* is typical of these.

Cultivation *Fuchsia* require a humid atmosphere and, when growing strongly, need plenty of water and a minimum temperature of 10°C (50°F). Under ideal conditions they can be almost perpetual-flowering, with a flush of flowers followed by a lull. It is best to reduce their water during late summer/autumn so that the woody stems can mature. Pruning to shape can be done during the winter. Hard cutting back will encourage plenty of flowering wood later. On established plants, remove some compost from the top of the pot at this time, replacing the worn out material with fresh. Give the woody stems a daily spray over; do not water the pots heavily for several weeks until the young shoots are growing strongly. When three pairs of leaves have formed, nip out the ends of all these growths to encourage the development of a bushy plant. Feeding can be done at 2-weekly intervals. *Fuchsia* root easily from soft cuttings placed in moist sand — or even water. Pot them up into a sandy loam compost with added peat and sieved well rotted cow manure if available.

Gardenia (Rubiaceae)

Description   For several reasons, *G.jasminoides* (Cape jasmine) is difficult to grow indoors, although, given patience, it is worth the attempt. In this species, the pale flowers always stand out in marked contrast to the shining evergreen leaves. *G.jasminoides* 'Professor Endz'* is a large-flowering kind with shiny green leaves narrowed to both ends, arranged either in opposite pairs or threes. The flowers are double, with glistening white petals, deepening to ivory as they age. They are delightfully fragrant and develop from solitary terminal buds from mid-winter to spring.

Cultivation   Constant year-round warmth is essential, together with a moist atmosphere when buds and flowers are being carried. Minimum temperature is 13°C (55.5°F). *Gardenia* will tolerate less warmth but higher temperatures are needed for growth and flowering. As foliage plants they would be satisfactory in the shade. For flower bud initiation they demand good light and a day-time temperature of 18°C (64.5°F). Under these conditions, most flowers will appear during spring but odd blooms occur at other times. Keep the compost moist throughout the year. Feed at 2-weekly intervals using a dilute organic-based material. Loam-less compost is ideal. Young plants, 2–4 years of age, are the best for flowers. Increase from soft cuttings in spring to enable a long season of growth before flowering the following winter.

90

Gerbera (Compositae) Transvaal daisy

Description   These tufted herbaceous perennials have upright, fairly narrow, lobed leaves, grey-felted beneath. The long, leafless flower stems terminate in a large daisy-like flower. In the wild form, which is sometimes seen in cultivation, these flowers are single and rich orange-red; cultivated sorts vary from yellow or white to pink and even dark red and there are splendid double forms* in which the central disc is filled with neatly radiating petals. Although naturally summer-flowering, *Gerbera* may flower at almost any time of the year, depending on the prevailing conditions. The blooms are particularly long-lasting.

Cultivation   *G.jamesonii* (Transvaal daisy), particularly in its cultivated forms, makes a charming indoor flowering pot plant for a warm, light, inside window, minimum temperature 7°C (44.5°F). Please also note that, for the plants' comfort, an upper temperature limit of about 24°C (75°F) is desirable. As these are almost hardy, dry air coupled with heat prove particularly debilitating for them, flagging leaves being the danger sign. Should this happen, move them to a cooler position until the weather changes. Water freely during their active growing period; keep the compost fairly dry at other times. Monthly liquid feeding will promote growth and flower production. A sandy loam compost suits these but it must be well drained. New plants can be raised from seed or by dividing up the crowns of established plants very early in the year.

Grevillea (Proteaceae)

This large exclusively Australian genus, numbering nearly 200 species, was named in honour of Charles F. Greville (1749–1809), a founder of the Royal Horticultural Society.

Description   All *Grevillea* are evergreen and extremely variable in both stature and appearance, ranging from mere creeping shrubs or bushes to large trees. Surprisingly, the popular indoor plant, *G.robusta* (Silky oak), is one of the largest. A native of Queensland and New South Wales, adult trees can be seen towering 30 m (98½ ft) or more, marking the paths of streams or low, presumably damp, places. Masses of yellow flowers are carried early in the year in dense one-sided racemes but, unfortunately, only on plants over 25 years of age. Youngsters grown indoors develop into upright plants of 1–3 m (3¼–9¾ ft). In Silky oak, the leaves are finely cut, fern-like, silver-backed and silky soft at first, later becoming dark green. *G.*'Robin Hood'* displays its red flowers against fern-like leaves. Use them in pots or tubs as individual specimens.

Cultivation   Grow *Grevillea* in a light airy position; minimum temperature 10°C (50°F). Do not overwater the pots but rather allow the compost to become partially dry each time. When feeding, use a deodorised natural fertiliser based on fish and blood, and amply diluted, at monthly intervals during the growing season. Any well drained acid (lime-free) compost suits them. Silky oak is increased from seed, others from cuttings.

Guzmania (Bromeliaceae)

This genus of bromeliads — relatives of the pineapple, comprises nearly 100 species of mainly epiphytic plants from Central and South America. Invariably attractive, particularly when about to flower, *Guzmania* are possibly more exacting in their requirements than similar plants, due to the moist heat required for much of the year.

Description   *G.lingulata minor* (Orange star)* is a smaller-grower than most *Guzmania*, forming clustering rosettes of thin, narrow, yellow-green, strap-shaped leaves. These are stemless, sheathing at their bases to form a water-holding vase. The central leaves become brightly coloured when flowering is imminent, the spike arising from the centre of the plant. In this species, orange-red bracts protect the cluster of white flowers within. Before the flowering rosette dies, replacement leaf clusters appear to repeat the cycle.

Cultivation   Shade with warmth and humidity the year round are required and a minimum temperature of 15°C (59°F). Water freely, topping up the 'cups' with rain water as needed. Fertilise at 2-monthly intervals with half-strength liquid, applying this to the growing medium and the reservoir. Use a 'specially formulated' orchid/bromeliad mix for potting, usually kibbled fir bark with added peat and leaf mould, and charcoal to keep the medium sweet. Increase plants by detaching well developed 'pups' or offsets.

Gynura (Compositae) Velvet plant

Two species and a possible hybrid between them are the representatives in our homes of this Asian genus, which contains some shrubby as well as herbaceous plants. They are wild in moist tropical regions and are consequently half-hardy, easily damaged by frost. These low-growing, perennial herbaceous plants are intriguing on account of their highly decorative leaves and stems, all of which are embellished with a dense velvet-like pile of soft, purplish hairs.

Description   The leaves are alternate, i.e. one at each node, and are either toothed or lobed. The orange flowers appear either singly or in corymbs (little clusters) at the ends of the branches during the winter or spring. Although quite pretty the flowers are foul-smelling and we suggest nipping them off before they have had time to open. In the Javanese *G.aurantiaca* (Velvet plant), the toothed fleshy leaves are ovate, fairly wide, with not only the leaves but also the stems densely coated in purple hair. The younger leaves are the more decorative, particularly as these also show red veins. *G.bicolor* (Oak-leaved velvet plant) has its thick leaves deeply lobed in the characteristic oak-leaf pattern.These have a dark green upper surface yet are purple-downy beneath. The orange flowers are composed simply of upright tubular disc florets. *G.* 'Sarmentosa' (*G.aurantiaca* × *bicolor,* Purple passion vine)* is bushy at first, later, unless supported, tending to scramble rather than actually climb. Soon the plants develop reddish stems and, as in the other species, their leaves are covered in fine purple hairs. In some lights they can appear to be reddish-purple beneath. This kind came originally from India and is also known as *G.scandens* or *G.procumbens.*

Try these unusual plants in a hanger where the light shining through the hairy leaves is most effective.

Cultivation   These plants should be grown in an airy spot with either a sunny aspect or light shade, preferably the former in order to promote the best colouring, minimum temperature 10°C (50°F). Warm conditions are essential when the plants are dormant for in cool humid weather the leaves can become mildew infected and will then rot easily. Water the pots frequently as required for the plants flag alarmingly in hot weather. Aphids can be a problem, especially on plants weakened by sporadic watering. Ours grow in standard soil-less compost. A mixture of sandy loam and peat is also suggested. Increase by taking tip cuttings which can be rooted in moist sand at almost any time material is available. Individuals tend to become top heavy or straggly unless the growing tips are repeatedly taken out to make the plant 'break''. Even old cut-back specimens will grow away strongly with renewed vigour following this treatment.

Hedera (Araliaceae) Ivy

The cultivated ivies are well known self-clinging evergreen climbers or trailers developed from species native to the northern part of the Old World. They are particularly valued for their ease of culture and speed of growth, as well as adaptability to a variety of indoor situations. Left alone, the pliable shoots attach themselves to supports by means of a mass of aerial roots. Sometimes we have to start them off by loosely tying them in the way we want them to go.

Description   Ivy leaves are leathery, usually lobed, although, in the many cultivars of *Hedera helix* (English ivy)*, leaf edges as well as colouring are extremely variable. It is interesting to note that the plant is sterile, not flowering in its creeping stage and only becoming fertile after reaching the top of its supports. At this point, the leaf edges change from lobed to entire; stems and branches become woody. Vegetative propagations from the adult growth retain this style, remaining erect and bushy. This phenomenon is, however, unlikely to be seen in the home. Cultivars include: *H.helix* 'Chicago' (Emerald ivy), one of the finest, with neat green five-lobed leaves; *H.h.* 'Curlilocks', with the margins of its green leaves deeply folded, a small bushy pot specimen; *H.h.* 'Glacier', a striking, silver, variegated plant with its neat, pointed leaf edges outlined in white; *H.h.* 'Gold Heart', with each of its dark green leaves displaying a bold golden blotch; *H.h.* 'Pittsburgh', another green-leaved form, this time having an extra long, pointed centre lobe.Ivies have several uses: as spreading cover either in planters or indoor gardens, trained up bamboo canes as room dividers, and individually or mixed in bowls or hanging baskets.

Cultivation   Ivies can be grown in sun or shade — the darker leaf forms accept shade as well as any plant; minimum temperature 5°C (41°F). Although reasonably tolerant of high day-time temperatures, ivies do best under cool conditions. Red spider mite can be particularly troublesome when the air is hot and dry. Although *H.helix* (Common ivy) is derived from a frost-hardy species, bear in mind that, when grown indoors, it will not be sufficiently hardened to survive frosting. Nor indeed will many of the bizarre leaf forms be suitable for outside culture. Any compost suits them; this should not be allowed to become dry at any time so just moist is the rule here. The propagation of these plants is by rooting cuttings. Most of the green cultivars will easily strike roots, even in plain water. Pot them up as soon as the roots form, for there is a danger of them rotting off before too long. Some of the yellow, variegated kinds do not make roots quite as easily. In this case try layering them into pots of sandy loam. Make certain that they have rooted before severing them!

Heliotropium (Boraginaceae) Heliotrope

The scientific name of this old-fashioned, cottage-garden flower comes from the two words *helios* (=sun) and *trope* (=turning). Nowadays, these little shrubs are called Cherry pie. The plants we grow are probably the result of hybrids between two Peruvian species, *H.peruvianum* and *H.corymbosum*. They are known as *H. × hybridum**.

Description A typical plant has long, ovate, pointed leaves, very wrinkled, dull green in colour. The flat or rounded inflorescence is composed of many starry, always delightfully fragrant flowers, held aloft on violet stems. Heliotrope make good little flowering pot plants.

Cultivation Place these plants in a light position indoors on a window ledge, with a minimum temperature of 8°C (46.5°F) where they will flower during the winter. Although not requiring too much heat at this time, they are very liable to frost damage — even a slight frost blackening the leaves. Heliotrope will grow in any light, well drained, fertile compost. Additional feeding may have to be done with care, as we have seen plants making leaves at the expense of flowers. New plants can be provided by rooting cuttings in moist sand in late summer. After potting these up, pinch out the growing tips to develop a stocky bush with plenty of flowers. The plants eventually become tall and rather sparse if left to develop naturally. The best specimens are those propagated every other year.

Hemigraphis (Acanthaceae)

This genus comprises about 20 annual and herbaceous species, all natives of Asia. The two mentioned below are valued in the home on account of their interestingly coloured leaves.

Description *H.colorata* (Waffle plant)* has stalked, opposite, oval leaves, heart-shaped at their base with rounded-toothed margins. The upper leaf surface, grey-green in colour, wine-red below, is marked with depressed veins. The tubular white flowers, with five spreading lobes, appear in short dense spikes from the leaf axils at the apex of the branches. These open in succession in summer and last for only a few hours. *H*. 'Exotica' (Purple waffle plant) is a quick-growing trailer with many branched stems, each having long inter-nodes. The ultimate branches carry large puckered-surfaced leaves, metallic grey above, rich purple below. Use either individually or as a group in a shady spot.

Cultivation For these plants to develop into fine specimens, conditions need to be warm and humid, minimum temperature 10°C (50°F). Their leaves colour well in the shade. Water freely in hot weather; keep the compost just moist at other times. Liquid feed can be applied to advantage; many foliage plants develop large healthy leaves as a result. Propagation by tip cuttings is easy. Sever these just below the node where rudimentary root buds can often be seen.

99

Helxine (Urticaceae) Mind-your-own-business

This genus, also known as Baby's tears and Irish moss, comprises a single completely ground hugging herbaceous species native to Corsica and Sardinia.

Description *H.soleiroli* (syn. *Soleirolia soleirolii*)* forms a dense prostrate mat of purplish threadlike stems clad with masses of tiny flattened, almost round, glossy green leaves. The green flowers are so tiny as to be insignificant. *H.s.* 'Aurea' is a slower-growing, particularly attractive, pale golden yellow-leaved version, requiring enough bright light each day to retain its distinctive colouring. These are particularly easy to grow, rapidly covering the surface of a pot or pan. Small patches may be started around the bases of other plants.

Cultivation These plants are for a cool spot indoors or out, part-shade for the green-leaved kind and an indoor minimum temperature of 5°C (41°F). They appreciate moisture, possibly preferring it in the air rather than having wet roots. For this reason, watering need not be too frequent in shady places, just sufficient to keep the compost moist the year round. Additional feeding should not be given. Better plants are the result, with their rooting stems hugging the soil, if this aspect of cultivation is purposely neglected. A well drained sandy loam compost is ideal. Increase your plants by division at any time or from tiny cuttings rooted during the summer.

Hoya (Asclepiadaceae) Wax flower

These belong to a large group of climbers and trailers, native to the East Indies, India, Malaya, China and Australia.

Description *Hoya* leaves are evergreen, usually thick with a shiny surface. The sweetly scented starry flowers develop in umbel-like clusters from spur-like appendages on the stem and are particularly long-lasting under cool conditions. *H.bella* (Miniature wax plant) forms a mass of pendant stems bearing small, pointed leaves and clusters of crimson-centred white flowers, chiefly under the leaves. *H.carnosa* (Wax plant)* is a popular climber, carrying its tough fleshy leaves in pairs on supple stems. These also bear the rounded, drooping clusters of pinkish-white waxy flowers each showing a red centre. Even young plants normally flower well, then can be trained over a simple wire hoop.

Cultivation These should be grown in diffused light, minimum temperature 10°C (50°F). Water generously during the early part of the year, but less as growth slows. Feed monthly during the period of peak growth. The compost for these plants should be open and free draining. Use turfy loam with peat, rotted manure and a sprinkling of sand, with a fertiliser such as hoof and horn meal or bone meal. Short cuttings of the previous season's wood, when rooted, will soon grow into useful plants.

Hypocerta (Gesneriaceae)

This small group numbers 15 or so species of small-growing shrubs from the tropics of Central and South America. Their name is compounded from *hypo* (= under) and *kyrtos* (= curved or humped), which refer to the pouch-like or swollen lower part of the corolla.

Description *H.radicans**, although a typical plant of the genus, is untypically adaptable for indoor cultivation — the others really need hot-house conditions in which to flourish. This species produces its pairs of bright, shiny green leaves on weak, floppy stems (the Latin *radicans* means creeping, rooting at the nodes) and the pouched orange flowers with five-part calyx and five tiny petals in turn develop from the leaf axils. Use these little plants with unusual flowers — once described as looking like feeding goldfish, trained over a tiny trellis.

Cultivation These plants require diffused sunlight, high summer humidity and a minimum temperature of 15°C (59°F). Watering entails maintaining year round moist compost, never over-wet. The leaves also need a misting over on all hot days. Liquid feed at monthly intervals, especially as new growth is being produced. A compost of loam, peat and sand, in the proportion 3 to 2 to 1, with added nutrients, can be used for potting. Propagation is by rooting stem or tip cuttings under close conditions in a greenhouse frame.

Hypoestes (Acanthaceae)

This is a large group of herbaceous plants and shrubs, some 150 in number, and all from Africa. They have undivided toothed leaves and tubular flowers in terminal spikes. The name comes from *hypo* (= under) and *estes* (= covered), as the bracts hide the calyx.

Description Originally from Malagasy, *H.sanguinolenta* (Freckleface) is a short, erect herbaceous plant with branched stems bearing small soft, dark green leaves intriguingly spotted and marked in pale pink. A cultivar of this species is mentioned in plant lists. Known as *H.s* 'Splash'*, this has larger leaves with a greater area of the dark green taken up by bold pink-red splashes. These are pretty foliage plants used as individual decorations in fairly dark places.

Cultivation These require warm humid conditions in semi-shade and a minimum temperature of 10°C (50°F). Water freely in hot dry weather, less when dull or cool. Freckleface plants respond well to foliar feeding sprays, often developing wider more colourful leaves. They are not long-lived in the home so it will be prudent to take a few cuttings each year. Trim back an old plant to secure these. Rooting them is easy. The youngsters produced from spring-rooted cuttings will, if pinched back on two occasions, soon fill a small pot. One more potting on and you will have fine plants for your home.

Impatiens (Balsaminaceae)

I.wallerana (Busy Lizzie)* belongs to a large genus represented in almost every continent. Our indoor plants originated in tropical East Africa. They are useful for indoor decoration and have been grown as such for many years.

Description Their branching stems are watery, glass-like, with long, ovate, glossy green or bronze, toothed leaves. The flowers, often profuse, are scarlet in colour, four-petalled and opening flat, each with a slender spur. They are carried singly or in pairs. Hybrids of the two natural variants, *I.w.holstii* and *I.w.sultanii,* have given us a wide range of colours from white through pink to red, purple and orange; there are also interesting bicolours. These make good plants both for the summer garden and indoors.

Cultivation *Impatiens* will grow either in sun or light shade, minimum temperature 7°C (44.5°F). Plenty of water must be given when the plants are flowering profusely, as well as a weekly feed with liquid fertiliser. Any compost is suitable, although one containing plenty of peat is best. Cuttings of the brittle, non-flowering stems root with ease — even in a glass of plain water placed in a light, warm spot. Pot these up as soon as they are rooted and discard old straggly plants. Pinch out the growing tips to encourage the plant to bush out.

Ixora (Rubiaceae)

This is a large group of evergreen shrubs and small trees of tropical origin. The name is derived from *Iswarra,* the name of a Hindu idol. Several species, and many natural varieties and hybrids, were among the more flamboyant of the tropical plants used to grace Victorian 'stove' houses. Today a few kinds are available as indoor plants.

Description *I.chinensis** from China and Malaysia is an upright grower, up to 1 m (3¼ ft) high, with slender, pointed, dark glossy green leaves. The flowers are salver-shaped, i.e. with a long slender tube and spreading lobes to the corolla. These are carried in globose corymbs or clusters. This is a variable species, the typical colour of the blooms is orange yellow. In the natural variety from Bengal, *I.c.rosea,* they are deep pink.

Cultivation These shrubs need high temperature plus constant moisture in the air; minimum temperature 16°C (61°F). Water generously in hot weather and mist over the leaves regularly. Drier conditions are needed during the winter rest period. Once established, the plants may remain in their pots for several seasons; liquid feed at 2-weekly intervals during the growing season. In pots, the plants have a compact bushy habit. Use a peat/sand mixture for potting and a sand/peat mixture for rooting short jointed cuttings of firm wood in spring. Keep 'close' until well rooted.

Jasminum (Oleaceae) Jasmine

This genus of shrubs and climbers, which numbers over 200 species, contains a few kinds grown indoors. The name derives from *Yasmin,* the Persian name for the plant.

Description *J.polyanthum* (Pink jasmine)* is naturally a rambling shrub. Indoors it may be trained up a cane or when young around a loop of stout wire. After transfer to a larger pot, its stems can be directed over trellis. Its glossy, dark evergreen leaves are divided into four or five leaflets. Although basically winter-flowering, the blooms may appear from early autumn through to late spring. The flower is tubular with expanded star-like petals, white with a wine-red reverse, giving a pink flushed appearance to the open blooms. Flowering is profuse; the stems carry large trusses, even when the plant is still young.

Cultivation This species is easily grown, requiring only a light position out of direct sunlight and a minimum temperature of 7°C (44.5°F). Water freely when in vigorous growth, less during the cool months. Liquid feed when the plants are flowering and continue until growth ceases. Prune away unwanted shoots after flowering. Any compost is suitable for these climbers. Pots may be stood outside on fine autumn days to ripen the wood before the onset of winter. Cuttings taken during early spring will root easily and should flower during their first full season.

106

Lantana (Verbenaceae)

This large genus of evergreen shrubs and herbaceous plants has undivided, usually opposite leaves with flowers clustered in rounded heads. Individually each flower is small and tubular with five spreading lobes. Several hybrids have been raised — those of *L.camara* making a colourful addition to the range of glass-house and summer bedding-out plants. As indoor plants, *Lantana* remain in flower for perhaps 9 months of the year.

Description *L.camara* (Shrub verbena, Yellow sage)* is a shrubby plant, originally from the West Indies, with upright, sometimes tending to angle, rough prickly stems, clad with opposite, ovate, crinkled leaves with toothed edges. The flowers mostly change colour as they age, the outside rows becoming progressively darker.

Cultivation Grow in sun, minimum temperature 10°C (50°F). Allow their compost to become partially dry between each watering. Feed at 2-weekly intervals with an organic liquid manure. A suitable compost consists of 2 parts good loam, 1 part old manure and 1 part peat with enough sand added to the mixture to ensure sharp drainage. Propagate *Lantana* from cuttings of short new growth taken with a 'heel', a portion of older wood which comes away when the shoot is pulled downwards. Prune old specimens back and re-pot them in early spring. *Lantana* flower on wood of the current season.

Kalanchoe (Crassulaceae)

This is a very large genus numbering nearly 200 species of fleshy succulents, mostly from tropical regions and including both herbaceous plants and shrubs. It is frequently divided into two genera, *Kalanchoe* and *Bryophyllum*. The former does not produce plantlets on the leaves as does *Bryophyllum*. Those described are in their different ways each attractive, two for flowers, one for foliage, the other for interest. For these reasons, *Kalanchoe* make a valuable addition to the range of good things we can grow under normal conditions in the home.

Description *K.blossfeldiana** is outstanding for its brilliant winter colour. It forms a short upright branching plant with thick fleshy dark green leaves. The flower clusters produced over most of the winter months are composed of many tiny starry blooms. These showy plants, originally from Malagasy, exhibit colours ranging from yellow, orange and pink through to the scarlet of the wild plant. As short-day-flowering plants they require a minimum of twelve hours continuous darkness in order to initiate their flower buds. *K.daigremontiana* (syn. *Bryophyllum daigremontianum*) is an erect grower with fleshy, toothed, long triangular brown-green leaves, red-edged when grown in good light. The interesting feature of this species is the manner in which many new plantlets appear along the serrated leaf edges. *K.manginii* is a wiry branched shrub with small, rounded, fleshy green leaves and loose clusters of drooping bell-shaped orange-red flowers. It is suitable for basket planting if several individuals are used for each basket. *K.tomentosa* (Panda plant) is very easy to grow and valued on account of its overall plush-like silver covering. It is upright with thick oval leaves, densely coated with short, soft, white hairs. The leaf margins are indented and marked with brown

Cultivation Although requiring a light airy position, the plants should be placed out of the direct rays of the sun with a minimum temperature of 10°C (50°F). Water is required throughout the year. Keep the compost constantly moist during hot weather, but water less when cool. Compost can be made from 3 parts loam, 2 parts peat and 1 part sand, together with added fertiliser. Propagate from seed sown during the early spring, cuttings (of the flowering kinds) or leaf-cuttings, i.e. detached leaves laid on sand.

Lilium (Liliaceae) Lily

The lilies are an important group of about 80 species of bulbous, herbaceous plants, native to various temperate or sub-tropical parts of the world but particularly Europe, Japan and California. They make splendid temporary indoor subjects.

Description The lilies used indoors have leafy erect stems and the leaves are shiny and strap-shaped. The generally large to very large flowers are various trumpet-shapes, sometimes with reflexed petals, often delightfully scented. Colours vary, frequently white or orange but pink to purple shades as well, often daintily spotted. *L.auratum* (Gold-rayed lily), *L.longiflorum* (Easter lily) and *L.speciosum* are recommended. Mid-century hybrids, as well as *L.* × *umbellatum**, are well known.

Cultivation Select a cool, partly shaded position. Minimum temperature is 8°C (46.5°F). The compost should be evenly moist at all times. Pot the bulbs in autumn, using a freely drained, humus-rich compost of loam, leaf mould, rotted manure and sand. Bulb fibre lacks nutrients and is not suitable for lily culture. Place them in a cool position until the shoots are well through then, after plenty of roots have formed, bring them into a light warm place for flowering. Afterwards, they can be put outside. Re-pot the bulbs into fresh compost each year. Propagation from seeds or detached scales is also possible.

110

Manettia (Rubiaceae)

Within this large group of evergreen plants from the tropics there is at least one which can be easily grown indoors.

Description   Introduced from Brazil in 1843, *M.bicolor** is a climber or twiner lasting long in flower. The thin, eventually stiff, stems are clad with opposite, lanceolate, light green leaves which taper to a point. As the stems elongate, stalked flowers appear in the leaf axils. These are tubular, bright red with a yellow tip, each held in a four-part calyx. On close inspection, the corolla is found to be yellow but with the lower part densely covered in bright scarlet bristles, giving a bicolour effect. These respond well to training around the inside of a window but support is needed because the stems are not self-clinging.

Cultivation   Grow in diffuse to bright light situations, minimum temperature 10°C (50°F). Keep the compost just moist in the cooler months. More liberal watering can be done at other times. Pot them up in loam, peat and sand; 1 part of each. Our own specimen is planted in a soil-less mix of 50/50 peat and pumice sand and receives a 2-weekly liquid feed from spring until autumn. Propagate by inserting half-ripe cuttings into moist sand. Cover them with a plastic bag then put into a warm, light spot out of direct sun for rooting to take place.

Maranta (Marantaceae) Prayer plant

This group of eight tropical American species contains plants suitable for indoor culture; their particular beauty lies in their splendidly marked leaves. The generic name, from which the family name is derived, was given in honour of the 16th century Venetian botanist, Bartolomea Maranti. The arrowroot of commerce is produced from the starchy tubers of *M.arundinacea* and closely related species.

Description *M.bicolor* is a stocky evergreen perennial plant having smooth elliptic leaves, dark green in colour with olive-green and grey markings and a dull purple flush beneath. The foliage is spreading during the day with the leaves open and flat. During darkness or dull weather, these fold shut from the mid-rib and are then held more upright. *M.leuconeura* var. *kerchoveana** is one of at least three, possibly four, natural variants (or possibly cultivars) of *M. leuconeura*. As in *M.bicolor,* these also have the habit of folding their leaves in 'prayer' at night. In *M.l.* var. *kerchoveana* the leaves are light green, each with a row of chocolate-coloured marks either side of the mid-rib. They are additionally blotched or spotted red beneath. *M.l.* var. *massangeana,* another Brazilian plant, has green leaves with a dark green central area and silver and deep pink lines extending from the mid-rib to the leaf margins.

Cultivation As room plants these must be put into a drought-free shady place, if possible in company with other shade-loving plants. Here the relative humidity is high, a condition which these plants enjoy. Minimum temperature is 12°C (53.5°F) or higher. Ample water must be provided during warm weather; the frequency of watering should be regulated according to the prevailing weather. Additionally, during their growing season, a light overhead spray with tepid water will keep the leaves looking fresh and healthy. When these curl or roll up during the day it is a sign that the air surrounding them is either too cold or too dry. Liquid feeding at 2-weekly intervals is beneficial during the growing season. Compost should be made from turfy loam and peat in equal parts, with sand added to promote free drainage. They also grow well in a compost of peat with added nutrients. *Maranta* are best grown in small pots big enough to take the roots comfortably without curling them over. Try re-potting them each spring; you will be certain of always having fine vigorous plants! Propagation is by carefully dividing the crowns during re-potting.

112

Microlepia (Davalliaceae)

This is a genus of ferns, numbering perhaps 45 species, considered by some authorities to be a subgenus of *Davallia*. The name *Microlepia* comes from *micros* (=small) and *lepis* (=scale), in reference to the tiny scale-like indusia (the membranes covering the sporangia which contain the spores). The appearance of the various members of the genus varies considerably. Some are tiny, reduced in all their parts, others comparatively large. Even the leaves span a range of shapes and textures from leathery entire (smooth-edged) to finely dissected, almost paper-thin.

Description *M.hirta* (syn. *M.speluncae* var. *hirta*)* is the *M.speluncae* of nurserymen. This is a bold and handsome fern for a large warm room or indoor garden. The broadly triangular fronds are two or three times pinnate with the final segments lobed or toothed. The light green of the emerging frond changes to dark green as it ages; the surface is scattered with short white hairs. This is an herbaceous species attaining 1 -1.5 m (3¼-5 ft) in height. They are native to parts of India, Sri Lanka, Malaysia and Polynesia. *Davallia canariensis* (Hare's foot fern), so-known because of the appearance of the creeping silver-hairy rhizomes, is a very pretty plant originally from the western Mediterranean, including Spain and the Canary Islands. Indeed this is the only one of the genus to be found in a wild state in Europe; the others are more likely to be seen in the tropics. This species makes a charming low-growing pot plant. Alternatively they can be planted in a hanging basket and, being virtually hardy, will succeed in a cool window the year round. The delicate fronds are well divided, cut almost to the central rib in the final segments and a light fresh green in colour. Of course, the rhizomes which spread over the pot sides remain a talking point.

Cultivation These two ferns, although widely different in appearance, both need a position in well diffused sunlight or part shade, minimum temperature 10°C (50°F). The temperature can go below this when plants of *Microlepia* are dormant. *Davallia canariensis* is also content with rather less heat. Humidity must be high for both species in warm weather. Keep the compost in their pots evenly moist the year round; even the deciduous plant should not be allowed to dry out when dormant. Ferns never require heavy feeding — a periodic scattering of time-release granules will be in order for established plants; youngsters can have half-strength liquid feeding at 2-monthly intervals. For potting up, use a mixture of lumpy peat and leaf mould with a little sandy loam added. The ferns dislike being potted 'hard' in a loamy mix. The species of *Microlepia* described can be increased from spores and division in early spring. Hare's foot fern can have its creeping rhizomes severed.

114

Monstera (Araceae)

This genus of nearly 50 species of evergreen climbers occurs naturally in the tropical regions of the West Indies and from Central to South America.

Description Although eventually very large indeed, *M.deliciosa* (Mexican breadfruit or Swiss cheese plant)*, bears attractive foliage, developing well in the home. The growth of the plants is particularly bold with thick, close-jointed round stems and leathery leaves very nearly heart-shaped in form. These leaves are highly glossy and deeply slit, as though cut by scissors. From the stems hang brown, cord-like, aerial roots, branching only when they find the moist soil for which they search. Unless the tops of very old plants have been used to provide the propagating material for your plants their flowers are not often seen in the home. They are of typical aroid shape, very large and ivory in colour, becoming yellowish and sweetly scented. After the spathe falls, the spadix enlarges, then, under ideal conditions, develops into the 'fruit' which gives rise to another common name — Fruit salad plant. To some this combines the flavours of pineapple, melon and peach. In its very young stage this plant is sometimes labelled *Philodendron pertusum* by nurserymen.

Use *Monstera* as a bold decorator plant — perhaps to clothe a wall in a foyer or as a feature in a large indoor garden.

Cultivation Indoor-grown specimens of this plant require shade and a minimum temperature of 13-15°C (55.5-59°F). to thrive. Established plants tolerate occasional very light frosts in those countries where they are traditionally grown out of doors. Although requiring abundant water during warm weather when in full growth, they also require good drainage to ensure that all surplus is removed before it has time to stagnate. Tell-tale brown leaf edges warn that something is amiss; either the compost is too wet and the roots are starting to rot, or the plants are suffering intolerably dry air conditions. Hosing over the leaves rather than a gentle misting may be the only way to moisten their massive leaves during hot weather. Sponge regularly to keep them dust-free rather than using large amounts of water. They are gross feeders and it is difficult to give them too much liquid feed at the normal dilution. Do not, however, be tempted to increase the strength but rather increase the frequency of application. Once each week is normal for our own plant. Loam-less compost is fine for *Monstera* but it must be lime-free. The alternative is peat and loam mixed together. Propagation is by rooting a portion of an old plant: either shoot ends or a section of stem bearing at least one good bud. This will be hidden down in the sheath at the base of the leaf stalk. It is usual to reduce the leaf surface area before inserting the cutting into a sand bed for rooting. Remember that these are tree climbers by nature, reaching 6 m (19¾ ft) or more in the wild. Sturdy supports are best provided while the plants are still immature.

116

Nephrolepis (Oleandraceae) Ladder fern

This genus of ferns, which numbers nearly 40 species, is widely dispersed throughout the tropics. Their name is derived from the Greek *nephros* (=kidney) and *lepis* (=scale), in reference to their under-leaf, kidney-shaped indusium — the covering for the spores — the first stage of the ferns' reproductive system.

Description *N.exaltata* in its various forms is surely one of the most popular of all ferns grown in greenhouses and as room plants. From the introduction of the original specimens nearly 2 centuries ago very many, perhaps 100, different varieties and cultivars of this species have been brought into cultivation. These range from plants resembling the wild species, with rather stiff, fresh green fronds, which are simply pinnate, to those with a lesser or greater degree of ruffling to the edges of the pinnae. Typical of the first group is the long-grown *N.e.* 'Bostonensis' (Boston fern). This is a tufted plant with long, naturally drooping fronds with almost flat, closely set pinnae. *N.e.* 'Fluffy Ruffles' is the other extreme. This is a dwarf plant of compact growth, its crowded upright fronds each with cut pinnae and frequently congested. *N.e.* 'Maasi'*, a cultivar raised in Europe, has a neat manner of growth with each broad frond carrying fresh green, rather long, waved pinnae. All are rapid growers, often thriving in situations where few other plants will grow. We once advised that these should be selected for a position in a hospital corridor. Here the plants did well under total artificial light. They make little root. Thin runners spread out from the crown in all directions. Under suitable conditions these develop buds along their length which eventually grow into fresh plants.

Use Ladder ferns for hanging baskets, which they will fill completely, as individual specimens or as ground cover for large planters.

Cultivation These ferns grow in filtered sunlight or light shade. High humidity does not appear to be a requirement although a draught-free position is. Minimum temperature is 10°C (50°F). Water the plants freely during the summer, or when the air is hot, and keep the compost just moist at other times. Feeding with organic-based liquid fertiliser at monthly intervals when your plants are growing well will be to their continued advantage. A compost of 1 part each of loam, peat and sand can be used for potting on. A little bone meal can be incorporated for base nutrient. Increase the named kinds of Ladder fern by dividing up the crowns which develop on the spreading rhizomes. A plant may need to be plunged in to a large container of moist peat for several months in order to develop roots prior to division.

Pandanus (Pandanaceae) Screw pine

This large genus contains both upright shrubs and trees. Some are valued as room plants, being highly ornamental when young. The botanical Latin name is from *pandang*, the Malayan word for the plant. Their common name derives from the spiral or screw-like dispersion of the leaves around the thick stem and 'pine' because of their superficial resemblance to the pineapple plant, pines being the early name for these. Screw pines are mostly plants of the marsh or sea-coast in Malaysia, Polynesia and tropical Australia, as well as the islands of Africa, where they grow wild. The seeds of certain species are said to be cooked and eaten and their leaves are used for weaving hats and baskets. *P.utilus* (Pandanus palm), from Malagasy, was once, and maybe still is, cultivated for its leaves which were used in the manufacture of sugar bags.

Description When mature these plants vary in size from about 1 m (3¼ ft) to over 10 m (32¾ ft) tall. The trunks frequently fork and, like other tree denizens of the marsh, they form aerial roots, an adaptation to withstand flooding. Young specimens are the only ones of any use as room plants. These are tufted with long, sometimes broad, leaves, linear in outline, frequently with toothed margins and basal mid-rib. *P.baptisii* (Blue screw pine) develops a dense symmetrical crown of long, slender, dark green, channelled leaves lined with thin white stripes. Each leaf ends in a slender point and in this species the margins are spineless. *P.veitchii* (Veitch's screw pine)* is a splendid indoor plant which forms a spiralled crown of leathery leaves. These are particularly bright shiny green, broadly margined with white, upright with recurved tips, the edges armed with white spines. Use the various members of this genus as bold feature or accent plants.

Cultivation Select a position in light shade, minimum temperature 15°C (59°F). Remember that these naturally inhabit wet places. The amount of water actually given has to be regulated according to the prevailing temperature. Additionally a period of winter rest should be induced by deliberately with-holding water during that season. Water must be sprayed over the leaves on hot days only. Young plants will have enough nutrients available to them in their compost. Older specimens can be side-dressed in the spring using a small amount of organic fertiliser. For re-potting, a mixture of sandy loam and leaf mould produces the correct medium for good root action. There is a tendency for the plants to push themselves out of their pots due to the direct downward thrust of the roots and this may mean an annual re-potting, using pots scarcely any bigger than the ones they are in at the time. Pot them with the base of the leaf rosettes high — i.e. well proud of the compost surface as they rot off rather easily if water lodges in the base of their leaves for too long. Some of the offsets which develop at the base of the leaf rosettes may be detached and used as cuttings. Remove these with the point of a sharp knife, placing them in pots of moist sandy loam. Keep them nearly dry until well rooted, watering them only from the base. Partly rooted suckers or seeds are other ways of perpetuating your stock.

Pachystachys (Acanthaceae) Candle plant

This is a small genus of woody herbaceous plants from the West Indies and South America.

Description *P.lutea** is a valuable addition to the range of easily grown indoor plants. They are bushy perennials, their stiff upright stems bearing long, ovate, pointed, dark green leaves. The flower heads, which appear at the apex of each stem, are hop-like in shape with the overlapping bracts coloured bright yellow. The flowers themselves are white, tubular, contrasting well with the rich hue of their holders.

Cultivation Light shade is preferred, to avoid the sun scorching the thin leaves, minimum temperature 10°C (50°F). Water liberally when in active growth but only a little when dormant. Regular feeding early in the year will be repaid with a bushy plant covered at first with fine foliage then later smothered in flowers. These plants seem to succeed in any normal well drained compost if their feeding requirements are met. Cuttings root readily and should have their growing points removed to encourage bushiness. The early flowers can also be cut off as they form. Attention to these details will result in a well proportioned specimen. Plants are first purchased either as large rooted cuttings early in the season or at point of flower. Many people maintain a young vigorous stock by pruning back old plants in mid-winter, then rooting the resulting shoots in order to continue the cycle.

Pellionia (Urticaceae)

Description These low, spreading plants have fleshy, succulent stems and comparatively large, thin, oval leaves; the flowers are insignificant in small heads. The interest for gardeners lies also in the most unusual colouring of the foliage. The stems of *P.pulchra* are clothed with pointed oval leaves, grey-green in colour, with an open network of darkish brown-green veins, giving a marbled effect. *P.repens* (syn. *P.daveauana)** has violet, dull-surfaced, dark green leaves, each with a broad irregular band of bright green. Use these unusual foliage plants in a hanging basket where their stems can hang down to display the leaves to their best advantage.

Cultivation Site *Pellionia* in a warm, humid shady place, minimum temperature 13°C (55.5°F). Water the pots freely only in hot weather but do not allow them to become parched at any time. Hot weather excepted, these plants must be watered with extreme care. The foliage must be dry overnight because water lodging in the leaf axils will cause the stems to rot through completely during one cool night. Liquid feed each month during the growing season. Plant either in standard soil-less compost or in a mixture of 3 parts loam, 2 parts sand. New plants come easily from cuttings or divisions. As with older stock, water the youngsters with great care.

123

Pelargonium (Geraniaceae)

This genus comprises 250 species found as wild plants in southern Africa. Their Latin name comes from *pelargos* (= stork), for in most kinds the fruit has a 'beak' which to some extent resembles that of the bird. Many of the horticulturally desirable plants, such as the popular geraniums, are hybrid in origin. Several make splendid indoor plants. Included with these, as well as geraniums, are the Regal pelargoniums, Ivy-leaved geraniums and other sorts, both hybrids and species, with delightfully scented leaves. All are perennials with rather succulent young shoots which frequently become woody as the plant ages.

Description The present day kinds of the colourful *P.* × *domesticum* (Regal pelargonium, Show geranium)* (bottom) are the result of hybridising at least three species. They develop into bushy plants bearing rounded flower heads. Individual blooms are often large, single or double, self or bicoloured, frequently with their petals wavy-edged. Their main floral display occurs from late winter to late spring. After flowering, trim their stems back then later stand the pots out of doors for the woody stems to ripen in the sun. *P.* × *hortorum* (Zonal, Bedding or Fancy-leaf geranium)* (middle) is a popular bedding-out plant, generally bushy in shape with succulent stems and round leaves. These are often marked with a horse-shoe-shaped, chocolate-coloured zone. The rounded flower heads are displayed in many shades of red, purple, pink and white depending on the cultivar selected. Attractively patterned leaves are also a feature of some kinds. *P.peltatum* (Ivy-leaved geranium)* (top), when grown naturally, is a low spreading plant, its prostrate stems furnished with thick ivy-shaped leaves. For indoor decoration the plants should be placed in a hanging basket where the rounded heads of single or double blooms are displayed to perfection.

Cultivation A light airy position is generally best for the flowering plants of this group, although part shade is tolerated; minimum temperature 7°C (44.5°F). Most benefit from being placed out of doors in a warm sheltered spot for at least part of the year. This treatment ensures that their stems are well ripened before the onset of cooler days. Water the plants freely when the weather is warm and growth progressing. The pots must be kept almost dry in the winter if the plants are semi-dormant. Geraniums flower for most of the year, their winter and early spring display being the most appreciated indoors. All are generally easy plants to grow, thriving in a variety of potting soils. The main consideration here is to see that the compost is free-draining. Either re-pot the plants annually or remove a little compost from around the pot rim replacing it with fresh material Feeding at 2-weekly intervals when the buds are showing will help the plant at this time. The prompt removal of all the old flower heads is another necessary operation. Short tip cuttings taken from the current season's growth is the best way to increase or maintain your stock. Root these in moist sandy compost, pinching out the growing points once or twice as they develop.

124

Peperomia (Peperomiaceae)

This very large tropical genus of over 1,000 species contains many admirable small-growing plants suitable for indoor decoration. Their name comes from *piperi,* (=pepper) and *omorios* (=similar)—they are related to the peppers.

Description The plants cultivated in homes are either bushy or trailing perennials valued for their undivided, evergreen, often attractively patterned, leaves. All are fleshy or succulent to a degree. Some are covered in fine hairs. Additionally the flowers, crowded into upright, tail-like catkins, are interesting. *P.argyreia* (syn. *P.sandersii,* Watermelon peperomia) forms a very pretty bushy plant with red stems, each displaying a broadly ovate leaf, blue-green in colour and marked with radiating silver bands. *P.caperata* (Emerald ripple) is an attractive species, originally from Brazil, with short-stemmed, rounded or heart-shaped leaves, each dark green and deeply corrugated. The dainty flower spikes are greenish-white. *P.c.* 'Tricolor' is a choice variegated sort raised in cultivation with wide cream-margined leaves held on pink stems. *P.hederifolia* (syn. *P.griseo-argentea,* Ivy peperomia)* has almost round, thin, 'quilted' leaves, their dull green surface reflecting a metallic silver hue. *P.obtusifolia* (Pepper face or Baby rubber plant) is a long grown favourite with concave, rounded, shiny green leaves growing on succulent pink-striped stems. *P.scandens* is a useful basket plant as its thick fleshy stems can hang down to display their well spaced heart-shaped green leaves.

Cultivation Light shade with good humidity is required in bright sunny weather but, when dull or cool, good light is required to bring out leaf colouration; minimum temperature is 13-15°C (55.5-59°F). All have to be watered with care; their pots should be allowed to dry partially so that air can be admitted to the compost between waterings. With us, this seems to be the pattern even in summer, although some kinds droop alarmingly in dry air conditions. Feeding may be carried out monthly using a half-strength dilution. An open gritty compost suits them well, or use a loam-less formulation. The plants may be kept in small-sized pots for several seasons. After re-potting, water the plants very sparingly for there is a real danger of stem rot quickly setting in. Propagation is by careful division of the crowns during the spring or, better still, by rooting cuttings of stems (trailing sorts) or individual leaves complete with a small portion of stem. These may be inserted in damp sand under a glass-topped box which is then put in a warm shaded place for rooting to take place.

126

Philodendron (Araceae)

This large genus of well over 200 species contains many members which, in their young stage, are extremely decorative indoor plants. The name *Philodendron* is derived from the words *philo* (=love) and *dendron* (=tree), alluding to the fact that most of the members of this genus depend on trees for their support. In the wild, a few of these are stemless; others are small trees. The majority of the kinds cultivated are, however, climbing shrubs. As with other genera in this family, they frequently pass through two distinct foliage phases, the juvenile form being the one seen indoors.

Philodendron are 'foliage' plants, i.e. the attraction of their foliage alone merits their inclusion in a collection of indoor plants. Some form of support will be needed for the plants from the time that they develop more than just a few leaves. The rapid-growing climbers, such as *P.oxycardium,* can be trained up a cane for use as a room divider. The large-leaved species need a stout mossed stick or tree fern stake for the aerial roots to grip on to.

Description *P.erubescens** is a most useful and decorative climber, the rooting stems clad with thick, leathery, arrow-shaped leaves, edged in red, then finally becoming deep green. *P.oxycardium* (Sweetheart vine, Cordatum) is a popular climber with shiny, deep green, broadly heart-shaped leaves. Tall-growing, it is said to prosper well in the steamy heat of bathrooms! *P.panduriforme* (Fiddle-leaf) is another climber, this time with dark olive-green leaves, each narrowed to the middle. *P.selloum* (Tree philodendron) bears a huge rosette of long-stalked, large, shiny green, deeply lobed leaves when young. A trunk slowly emerges with age. It is a very bold feature plant for the largest space.

Cultivation These favourite decorator plants grow in shade or diffused light; as the majority are tropical in origin they require a minimum temperature of 13-15°C (55.5-59°F). Water the plants freely during hot weather and administer an overhead spray to maintain high humidity. During cooler months, enough water to keep the compost moist is sufficient. Liquid feed may be applied at 2-weekly intervals when the plants are in active growth. A humus-rich compost of peat or peat and leaf mould in equal parts, plus added fertilisers, is the most suitable for these, originally forest-dwellers. Propagation is by cutting the old stem into segments, leaf cuttings — complete with bud, tip cuttings and layering. In the latter, layers may be pegged down into a pot of compost or treated as air-layers (mossed).

Pilea (Urticaceae)

This is a large widespread genus occurring in many tropical countries. The representatives grown as house plants have attractive foliage.

Description Excepting the Artillery plant, *P.microphylla,* which is of completely different appearance, the leaves are carried in pairs, ovate to rounded in shape, distinctly three-veined. *Pilea* flowers are small and carried in the leaf axils. *P.cardieri* (Aluminium plant)* is a bushy rather succulent-stemmed species from South-East Asia. Introduced into France from Indo-China in 1938, the whole stock now in commerce is said to be derived from these originals. The dark green leaves have silver-grey patches between the sunken veins and, from a distance, the leaves appear to be completely silver. A pink stemmed dwarf cultivar, *P.c.* 'Minima', smaller in all of its parts, is a charmer. *P.involucrata* (syn. *P.spruceana,* Friendship plant) is a leafy Peruvian species with thickset, spreading fleshy stems bearing oval, slightly toothed, rich bronze-green leaves patterned with grey. Each leaf is wine-red on the reverse. *P.microphylla* (Artillery or Pistol plant) is an upright grower with its glossy stems bearing masses of tiny, fresh green, fern-like leaves. The common name stems from the plant's habit of discharging clouds of pollen when the leaves are touched during dry summer weather. *P.* 'Moon Valley' is an attractive plant with toothed, wrinkled leaves, light green in colour and heavily marked with chocolate-brown. *P.repens* (Blackleaf panamiga) is a decorative creeping plant from Mexico with thin rounded leaves, glossy coppery-brown in colour with purple beneath. These plants may be used either as individual specimens or massed in a large container.

Cultivation Select a draught-free shady position for displaying *Pilea.* They also appear to be particularly susceptible to damage by coal gas fumes. The minimum temperature is 10°C (50°F). Water freely only when they are in active growth; the compost can be kept just moist at other times. An overhead spray with tepid water will be welcomed by the plants in hot weather but do not allow any water to rest on their leaves when it is dull or cold. Soil-less compost, provided that it is reasonably drained, will prove suitable for this group. Liquid feeding will be needed at monthly intervals 8 weeks after potting in this material. Propagation is by rooting the tip cuttings of the current year's growth. Take cuttings during the summer and pinch out the growing tips of the rooted plants occasionally in order to develop bushy specimens.

Platycerium (Polypodiaceae)

This genus of 17 or 18 species of epiphytic ferns numbers among its members a few which are suitable for use as indoor plants. They are of the most extraordinary appearance yet, at the same time, attractive, reminding one as they do of large pieces of nicely proportioned seaweed! The botanical name comes from a description of one of these leaves: *platys* (=broad) and *keros* (=horn). *Platycerium* fronds are of two very different shapes. The barren fronds are round and flat and occur at the base of the plant where they may be found clustering against its support. The spore-bearing fertile fronds are long, frequently very long, divided at their ends into stag's horn-like divisions. Where they occur naturally, growth is sometimes on moist rocks but is more often on the trunks or larger branches of trees. Here their spores find a place to lodge, eventually to develop first of all one circular disc, then a series, before themselves sending out the large fruiting fronds.

Description *P.bifurcatum* (syn. *P.alicorne,* Stag's horn fern)* is a popular, variable species from the tropics, including warm temperate parts of Australia. It has greyish, barren fronds and normally pendant, dark green, deeply divided fertile fronds. On adult specimens, young plants appear clustered around the roots. Once acclimatised, this species appears to be hardy outside in sheltered places where only light frosts occur. *P.b.* 'Netherlands' is a Dutch-raised cultivar of the Stag's horn fern with rather hairy broad fronds, well divided and held out at various angles from the base of the plant. *P.grande* (Elk horn fern) from tropical Asia and northern Australia is a fine house plant when young. With age, however, this species (under ideal conditions) can send out leaves approaching an incredible 2 m (6½ ft) in length, and naturally requires a large accommodation area! Their sterile fronds are rounded; the dark green, deeply lobed, fertile fronds which appear with age are both semi-erect and drooping.

Use these fascinating plants as individual specimens hung on a wall or in a hanging basket.

Cultivation *Platycerium,* being epiphytic, require high humidity plus shade at all times and a minimum temperature of 13-15°C (55.5-59°F). Under normal warm conditions, the plants should be kept moist throughout the year. Do not allow water to lodge in the overlapping disc-like fronds during cool conditions or they will discolour or perhaps even rot. These plants are frequently attached to a block of hardwood and the space behind their sterile fronds filled with moist peat. Alternatively the peat may be held in place with moss and the plant may be attached to that. Basket plants can be started in a mixture of coarse peat and leaf-mould with a little crushed charcoal added to keep the compost sweet. When they are produced, small plantlets on the roots offer a ready means of propagation.

Plectranthus (Labiatae)

This is a large group of mainly herbaceous plants, a few of which are cultivated as indoor plants. The name is derived from *plectron* (=spur) and *anthos* (=flower). Some species are noted for their pretty leaves. Others have attractive flowers. These are generally small- to medium-sized, sometimes stalked, nearly always in whorls of several blooms.

Description *P.australis* is a horticultural name for a species which is probably more correctly described as *P.verticillatus*. It is a native of Australia and several Pacific islands. This kind produces stems of attractive, small, smooth leaves with crenate (notched or scalloped) margins. The two-lipped flowers are small and white. *P.coleoides* 'Marginata' is a dense, compact, bushy plant with (comparatively) large, dark green leaves on four-angled stems. These leaves are shaded grey with the edges clearly outlined in creamy-white. As in the former species, the margins are also notched. This kind comes from southern India and has white and purple tubular flowers. *P.oertendahlii* (Prostrate coleus)* is a low, creeping species with rooting stems. The broad leaves are small, slightly hairy, green, netted with silver veins. The rounded, toothed leaf margins are purple-tinged, with older leaves having a decidedly purple cast to them. This is a most attractive kind for an indoor hanging basket. It has become popular only in recent years — especially in Scandinavia.

Cultivation Place your pots of *Plectranthus* in a warm humid position in light shade, minimum temperature 10°C (50°F). They require the compost to be constantly moist but never with 'wet feet'. Peak watering time will, of course, be in the growing season of spring and summer. Frequent liquid feed will be needed only during the first year. If loam-less compost has been used for potting, one application per month will be in order. Older plants, established in larger containers, can have a side-dressing of dry fertiliser watered in at the beginning of the season. They grow well in a light, rich compost of loam, leaf mould and old manure in equal parts and also in peat/sand mixes. Propagation from short stem cuttings is relatively easy. Root these in late summer, keeping them warm and moist until the new growth reveals that roots are forming. When well rooted, they can be potted off into single small pots; a further move during the following spring will have the plants ready for display. Removing the growing tips when the plants are tiny will encourage bushiness. Although this develops naturally later, it is best to make them 'break' at an early age.

Primula (Primulaceae)

This very large genus of perhaps 500 species contains many valuable garden plants. They are in the main native to the northern temperate regions. In addition to the garden favourites, such as Polyanthus, and other attractive sorts grown in alpine or woodland gardens, there are other, tender, species useful for an indoor situation. The name *Primula* comes from *primus* (=first), the European primroses and cowslips being the harbingers of spring.

Description Every *Primula* develops a basal rosette of leaves from which either individual stalked flowers or erect stems bearing many flowers are produced. Individually these are primrose-like in shape, although few indeed bear the same colour flowers as that delightful plant; most are in shades of pink, purple, red and white. An exception to this is *P. × kewensis* (*P. floribunda × verticillata*). This is a delightful hybrid with long, ovate, toothed leaves which are covered in farina. The sweetly fragrant, clear yellow flowers spring from the upright stems in separate whorls during the winter and early spring. *P. malacoides* (Fairy primrose) is a Chinese species with many rosettes of wavy-edged, stalked leaves — particularly hairy beneath. The small red, purple or white flowers which appear in succession are arranged in tapering whorls around the dainty upright stems. *P. obconica** is a very popular pot plant with rather brittle rounded leaves on long stems. The individually large blooms are produced in showy umbels or clusters held above the foliage. Their colours are pink, purple, red or white, usually centred with a yellow 'eye'. A word of warning! Both stems and leaves are furnished with irritating hairs to which some persons are allergic. *P. sinensis* (Chinese primrose) is normally a winter-flowering pot plant with bold, softly hairy, lobed leaves. The initial flowers appear down in the centre of the rosette of leaves then later, when their stout stem pushes up, they are carried in whorls. The flower colours in this species include brick red, pink, purple and white, once more with a contrasting 'eye'.

Primula are usually classed as temporary indoor-flowering pot plants. Use them as individual small specimens or massed in a planter.

Cultivation To develop satisfactorily, most *Primula* need moist, shady, cool conditions. The indoor kinds are no exception but do require more warmth than the hardy plants and a minimum temperature of 7°C (44.5°F). All should have plenty of water in hot weather and must not be allowed to dry out. Feed with liquid fertiliser at 2-weekly intervals when the plants are flowering to prolong their display. Remove the flower heads as they fade. A sandy loam compost with added peat is suggested. Although these are all perennials, for quality specimens, the raising of new plants annually from seed has much to recommend it. Fortunately this is a very easy group to germinate if the seed is fresh. Providing replacements should be within the scope of anyone with a basic seed-raising kit comprising seed tray, compost and a sheet of glass or domed plastic cover. Sow the fine seeds on to the surface of the prepared, pre-moistened compost during the summer. Prick out the seedlings directly into the small-sized pots they will occupy when flowering. Larger specimens can be grown by sowing the seeds earlier and giving the seedlings two moves instead of one.

Pseudopanax (Araliaceae) False panax

This small genus of shrubs and trees comprises six species — all evergreen. Although seldom seen as indoor plants outside their native New Zealand, some are nevertheless of value in large pots, planters or tubs. As well as their attractive leaves and form they are tough, adapting well, even under adverse, low light conditions.

Description The difference between juvenile and adult foliage is more marked in *Pseudopanax* than in other members of the family. The flowers are individually small and insignificant, greenish and followed by shining black berries. *P.arboreus* (Five finger) develops into a tree in the wild but is more familiar to gardeners as an upright-growing shrub. This carries large, glossy green leaves divided into five to seven short-stalked leaflets, each with coarsely toothed margins. In the wild, the flowers develop into large conspicuous bunches of decorative jet black berries. *P.crassifolium* (Lancewood) in its young stage, forms a thin, unbranched, vertical stem with rigid, sharply toothed leaves. These are long, normally pendant, dark green flushed with purple beneath. The mid-ribs are either red or yellow and hybrids, with a similar style of foliage, but bushier and much-branched, also occur. *P.laetus* is another plant with handsome leaves which could be confused with Five finger. In this species, however, the glossy green leaves are larger and divided into three lobes. *P.lessonii* forms a dome-shaped shrub when planted in a container. The leathery leaves are rounded, compound with three to five leaflets each, coarsely toothed or entire (leaves which are not notched) or perhaps toothed at the apex. The cultivar 'Gold Splash'* is a particularly bright addition to a well lit hall or covered porch, with large areas of its dark green compound leaves 'splashed' with yellow-gold. *P.lessonii* 'Purpureum' with its purple-tinged leaves we have another valuable colour break. The intensity of the colour depends on the amount of bright light received.

Cultivation These are adaptable plants growing in the sun or shade, minimum temperature 7°C (44.5°F), less if the roots and air are comparatively dry. Keep the compost just moist throughout the year. Stagnant wet conditions at the roots can be fatal during cool weather. Young plants should have their feed incorporated in the potting compost. Established specimens can receive a scattering of time-release capsules over the container surface or a top-dressing of fertilised compost. Thin or overcrowded shoots can be cut away during the winter. A few stout stems bearing large leaves should be the aim with this group. Treat any wounds with a grafting wax preparation in order to prevent the entry of disease organisms. Increase of the species is from seeds or cuttings. During the summer, take tip cuttings of soft wood of the cultivars of *P.lessoni* and good forms of *P.crassifolius*. This is a specialised process requiring the close humid conditions of a propagating case or mist bench.

Note: Some species of *Pseudopanax* are sometimes placed in the genus *Neopanax*.

Pteris (Pteridaceae)

This genus of ferns, containing approximately 250 species, is a cosmopolitan one. A dozen or so, mostly occurring in warm or tropical areas, together with their numerous forms and cultivars, are grown in homes and greenhouses. Among their numbers are some of the most useful, yet least demanding, of all the ferns. Their name comes from the Greek *pteron* (=a wing), and describes the form of the fronds. Many cultivars of the popular species have been developed. With their normal leaves altered in a most attractive way some of these are most desirable as indoor plants. Many of these could be termed 'old-fashioned plants' for they were much in demand during Victorian times when they were known as table ferns.

Description *P.cretica* (Ribbon fern) comes from places as far apart as South Africa, Japan and the USA (Florida). This is an extremely variable, always decorative, species with ribbon-like dark green fronds on erect wiry stalks. The leaflets are of two forms, sterile or fertile (spore-bearing); the latter are more narrow and on longer stems. *P.c.* 'Albo-lineata' is a most attractive dwarf variegated cultivar in which each leaflet displays a broad, central, white stripe. *P.ensiformis,* from tropical Asia and Australia, is a small-growing species of elegant appearance. The barren fronds are divided into several leaflets with lobed segments whereas the fertile fronds are tall, narrow with wavy edges, and bright green in colour. *P.e.* 'Victoriae'* is another dainty fern in which each leaflet is prettily variegated in white. *P.multifida* (Spider fern) is a popular fern long in cultivation. It received its familiar name by virtue of the long, spidery, widely separate leaflets. *P.tremula* (Australian bracken) can attain a large size when mature with heavily dissected fronds up to 1 m (3¼ ft) long. This is an herbaceous species of robust growth, its common name reminding us that the widespread Bracken fern, or Brake, is a close relative. Ferns have several uses in the home, particularly as individuals to decorate a shady spot. Most grow well in the moist air of the bathroom.

Cultivation Except for the shade-*loving* variegated species which, unlike almost all light-demanding variegated plants, actually develop better in the shade, others are fairly *tolerant* of strong light. Like virtually all ferns, however, they prefer the shade and require a minimum temperature of 7°C (44.5°F). A humid atmosphere is the ideal climate and can be provided either by growing the plants over a gravel-filled tray, kept constantly moist by adding water as it evaporates, or by plunging the pots into a container of moist peat. Within the pots, keep the compost moist without over-watering. Try to arrange a period over the winter months for the plants to rest under cooler conditions; they will be much better in the spring. A compost rich in humus made up from 2 parts peat, 1 part loam, 1 part sand will prove satisfactory. Propagation is by the division of the crowns or rhizomes whenever this is possible. Self-sown or deliberately sown spores germinate readily. We mention this because anyone who has grown these in a greenhouse with a weathered boiler-ash floor will know that they can become almost a weed!

Rhapis (Palmae) Lady palm

Of all living greenery which we can select to decorate interiors, the palms must be among the most noble, interesting and valuable plants. This great family contains over 1,800 species and is widespread throughout the tropics and subtropics. Generally speaking, palms produce two different styles of leaf: one group has fan-shaped leaves, divided into nearly equal-sized leaflets, which arise closely together at the extremity of a long stalk; the other has pinnate leaflets disposed along each side of a mid-rib and develops into a long arching frond; these can appear as feathery plumes. Although varying considerably in size, the stems or trunks of palms are all simple, i.e. unbranched, except for the Doum palm of the Upper Nile. Some are almost reed-like in the wild, struggling through dense vegetation towards the glimmer of light which penetrates the rain forest canopy. Some are dainty, sometimes developing into a small clump — but usually of low ultimate height. The giants of the family have stems of 50 m (164 ft) or more in height. Most palms, including those grown indoors, delight in both heat and moisture. Palms are material *par excellence* for the decorator, both private and commercial and are perhaps the best individual specimen plants we have.

Description *Rhapis excelsa* (Lady palm)* forms a clump of slender cane-like stems which carry leathery, dark green, palmate leaves. Among the other genera of palm there are several species suitable for indoor cultivation. *Caryota mitis* (Dwarf fishtail palm), a slow-growing species from South-East Asia, is an attractive plant, developing arching fronds with drooping fan-shaped leaflets. *Chamaedorea elegans* (Parlour palm) is a dainty-grower with one or more upright trunks, each topped by a cluster of dark green leaves. These are shade-lovers and need to be grown in moist, well drained pots. *Cocos weddeliana,* correctly *Syagrus weddeliana,* is one of the most graceful, with arching feather-like fronds deeply divided into many narrow leaflets. As small plants, these do well in an indoor terrarium where the extra humidity is appreciated. *Howeia belmoreana* (Sentry palm) is an indoor favourite for several reasons: it is highly decorative, quick-growing — yet manageable for many years, and tough and adaptable when grown in light shade. The long leaf stalks each end with a series of dark green, pinnate fronds neatly arrayed; when mature these leaflets droop in a most attractive manner.

Cultivation Indoors, most palms do best in either well diffused light or part shade, minimum temperature 10-13°C (50-55.5°F). Water them frequently, maintaining an even moisture content. Syringe the leaves often in hot weather. Young plants should be started in loam and peat, then, when well established, potted on; the humus content should be reduced each time. Eventually the potting soil can be just sandy loam. Pot firmly with the bases of the crowns just above the soil level. These are long-lived plants continuing well, even when remaining in small pots, i.e. small when compared with the bulk of the occupant. They will benefit from an annual top-dressing. Propagation from seed is feasible but seldom attempted in the home.

Rochea (Crassulaceae)

This small genus of succulents from South Africa has been in cultivation since 1710.

Description *R.coccinea* (syn. *Crassula rubicunda*)* has branched, upright, succulent stems with many crowded pairs of opposite, rather leathery, pointed ovate leaves. The bright scarlet, star-like, four-petalled flowers are arranged in false umbels (flat clusters) at the apex of each branch. Each is slightly fragrant.

Cultivation Select a well lit place where the plants will not get scorched by brilliant sun; minimum temperature 7°C (44.5°F). Although easy to grow, correct cultivation, particularly watering, will ensure better quality, more floriferous plants. When vigorous growth commences in early spring, water generously, keeping the compost moist at all times. Water less frequently when the flower buds appear, allowing the compost to really need water each time. Mist the flower buds over daily. After flowering, the pots can go outside for the summer. Keep the plants fairly dry during winter when they should be dormant. Prune old flowering stems back in early spring. Liquid feeding may be heavy during the *early* stages of spring growth — even at every other watering. For potting, use a mixture of 2 parts loam, 1 part peat, leaf mould or well rotted manure, 1 part coarse sand. Increase from seed or cuttings of side shoots started in late spring.

Rondeletia (Rubiaceae)

This large genus of shrubs from Central and South America, includes about 100 different species. Those cultivated have branched heads of small showy flowers, usually carried in dense terminal, but sometimes axillary, clusters. The genus was named by Plumier, the discoverer of *R.amoena,* in honour of Rondelet (1507-66).

Description *R.amoena** is an upright, branching shrub attaining over 2 m (6½ ft) when growing naturally — considerably less when used as an indoor plant, and fortunately flowering at a very early age. The leathery, evergreen leaves are pointed ovate, medium-brown and somewhat rugose (wrinkled) at first, carried in sessile or stalkless pairs. The small scented flowers are arranged in round clustered heads, each pink with a yellow eye. Use in a conservatory or suitably sited in a sun-room.

Cultivation These shrubs need a very light spot but out of the sun's glare, minimum temperature 10°C (50°F). Liberal amounts of water can be given but do not overdo this when the shrubs are dormant. To maintain the feeding element in the compost, top-dress established plants with fresh compost or use time-release granules. For re-potting, use a combination of loam, peat and sand. The plants are increased by inserting cuttings of half-ripe wood in the close atmosphere of a propagating case.

Saintpaulia (Gesneriaceae) African violet

There are 12 species in this African genus but all the diverse colour forms have been developed, particularly in the USA, as hybrids and cultivars of *S.ionanthe**. The generic name commemorates its discoverer, Baron Walther von Saint Paul-Illaire (1860-1910) of Berlin.

Description These plants are almost stemless, hairy perennials which form a dense mound of foliage. Their long-stalked, evergreen leaves are ovate in outline. The flowers are stalked, carried in a loose head which is itself on a short peduncle or stem. The original plants had wide, bell-shaped, single flowers, violet-blue in colour, each opening to display a central mass of golden stamens, and dark coppery-green leaves which were reddish beneath. As well as similar plants, today we find other colours, including white, pink, red, violet and purple, in single, semi-double and double form, some with fringed petals. These highly decorative small pot plants are virtually continuously flowering. They can, however, be classed as only moderately easy to grow and maintain. More often than not these are displayed as individuals. Where space permits, grouping — perhaps in a basket, can be most effective.

Cultivation African violets develop best in light shade with some degree of increased humidity. Some of the best plants we have seen were growing in bathrooms and kitchens, minimum temperature 13°C (55.5°F). The pots should be kept moist but on no account stood in water-filled saucers. Water must be kept off their leaves by watering the pots from below. Do allow the pots to drain through before replacing the pots in their covers. Regular liquid feeding may be done to advantage using dilute fertiliser at 2-weekly intervals at all times when the plants are in bloom. There are two main ways of increasing *Saintpaulia*: by leaf cuttings during the summer or dividing the dense crown in the spring. The former method is the more satisfactory. The fully developed leaves are detached, complete with a portion of leaf stalk. Holding the leaf upright, bury the stems until the base of the leaf is just resting on the surface of the moist sand. Rooting takes place best in a warm humid atmosphere. Do not, however, allow the sand to remain wet or rotting will occur. Most garden centres stock special growing mix for these plants. Use this for your young plants, potting them on when they are large enough.

Sansevieria (Liliaceae)

This genus of over 50 species comes from Africa and the East Indies and provides some attractive easily-grown plants. These are valued for the rosettes of leaves which offer both colour and a change in form from the majority of house plants. A limited economic demand exists for the fibre from the leaves of other species. The botanical name of the group was given in honour of Raimond de Sansgrio (1710-71), Prince of Sanseviero.

Description In most species the leaves are long to very long, developing from a thick creeping rhizome or underground stem. The flowers sometimes seen on established specimens are fragrant, greenish-white, in tapering spikes. These flowers can be followed by orange fruits. *S.hahnii* (syn. *S.trifasciata hahnii*, Bird's nest sansevieria) is a clump-forming species with rosettes of spirally arranged, broad ovate leaves, dark green in colour with lighter green bandings. In *S.h.* 'Golden Hahnii' indoor plant enthusiasts have a valuable sport or mutant form with its thick, broad, leathery leaves margined with a wide band of golden yellow. *S.h.* 'Silver Hahnii Variegata', has rather narrow spreading leaves which display silver bandings and a thin yellow edge, together with an overall silvery sheen. *S.trifasciata* (Mother-in-law's tongue plant, Snake plant) is a West African species, long in cultivation. The leaves are upright, sword-shaped, dark green in colour with wide grey bandings. *S.t.* 'Laurentii'* is now seen more frequently than the original species. In this cultivar, the leaf margins each bear a wide yellow stripe. In addition to their use as isolated specimens, they mix well with other plants. Here the narrow vertical-leaved species especially provide useful height without great width.

Cultivation A position in either sun or shade suits these adaptable plants. The kinds with yellow variegation require more light to bring out their particular feature. Minimum temperature is 12°C (53.5°F). If any difficulties arise over growing *Sansevieria* in the home, it must be over the question of watering. With the realisation that these are semi-succulent in nature, the problems should be limited. Except for the time of peak new growth, their pots can be allowed to become virtually dry before each thorough watering. They may also be allowed to become almost pot-bound before re-potting is needed. Select a sandy loam compost with a small amount of peat. Liquid feeding at 2-monthly intervals during the spring and summer will be adequate; try using foliar feed for these. Propagate either by dividing up the crowns at re-potting time (the *only* method suitable for named kinds) or from leaf cuttings. Cut the leaves into segments and push these into the rooting medium — remember which is their natural way 'up'! If these are placed in a warm propagator, a bud as well as roots will form at the base of the cut leaf. Before long a rosette of leaves will appear at the side of the old leaf portion.

Saxifraga (Saxifragaceae)

Of this large genus, which contains many pretty, mostly hardy alpine plants, only one is considered to be satisfactory indoors, the Japanese *S.stolonifera* (Aaron's beard)*.

Description Although their starry white flowers in summer are pretty enough, it is for their evergreen, long-stalked, rounded leaves that these plants are usually grown. The leaves are slightly hairy above, produced in loosely tufted rosettes, green marbled with silver, and purplish beneath. The plant forms numerous creeping red stolons (stems) bearing tiny new plantlets. *S.s.* 'Tricolor' is a small edition of the original species with leaves which are boldly margined in cream and, since the wine colour of the underleaf shows through, the effect is altogether charming. Remember that these plants are prone to sunburn if not positioned carefully and that water lodging in the crown causes rotting very quickly. Use small pots as edgings in an indoor garden; larger specimens can go in a hanging basket.

Cultivation These plants will tolerate sunlight to a degree but prefer a cool position, minimum temperature 4°C (39°F). Water freely when the temperature is high. Just moisten the compost at other times. Except when the plants are tiny, liquid feeding will only be required when using loam-less compost. For potting, a mixture of peat or leaf mould and sand is ideal. Propagate from the tiny plantlets produced on the ends of the runners.

150

Schlumbergera (Cactaceae)

This genus includes over 200 species of forest cacti from South America and was named in honour of Frederick Schlumberger, an amateur botanist. The species are characterised by their often bright green, flattened, leaf-like shoots, oval in outline with notched edges. The flowers, which hang from the upper axils of the cluster of well divided stems, have protruding stamens.

Description *S. × buckleyi* (Christmas cactus)* has the typical flat segmented stems arching outwards from the centre of the plant. Their long flowers, with reflexed outer petals are trumpet-shaped and bright rose in colour. These flower in the depths of the northern hemisphere winter. Use *Schlumbergera* in individual pots on a window sill, or in a hanger.

Cultivation While the plants are indoors, place the pots in a diffused light with minimum temperature of 10°C (50°F). Keep them just moist with the amount of water given them reaching a peak by the time the flowers appear. Use a weak solution of liquid fertiliser once each month during the summer. During this time, they may be stood out of doors in a partly shaded place. When re-potting, a humus-rich compost is needed; one containing at least half leaf mould will be welcomed by the plants. Increase is by inserting stem cuttings during the summer.

151

Schefflera (Araliaceae)

This genus belongs to the Araliaceae, or, as they were known at one time, the Ivyworts — Ivy or *Hedera* being a well known member of this family. The family as a whole is composed of over 600 species of diverse appearence. Several are almost indispensible as indoor plants and are described under the generic names: *Dizygotheca, Fatsia, Hedera.* Many name changes have occurred within this family over the years, including that of the principal plant described below. The name *Schefflera* commemorates J.C.Scheffler of Danzig.

Description *S.actinophylla* (syn. *Brassaia,* Umbrella tree)* frequently attains 20-30 m (65½-98½ ft) in its native Queensland, New Guinea and Java. Indoors they usually develop several slender grey trunks or upright branches ending in heads of large compound leaves. Individually these are long-stalked and terminate in a number of elongated ovoid leaflets, each on its pedicel or stem. The leaflets vary in number from three to fifteen and arise at the same point to radiate out and downwards rather like the metal ribs of an umbrella. Starting from one side of the leaf and working around, the leaflets increase in size, reaching a maximum before gradually decreasing in size once more. The large straight-stemmed panicles of wine-red blooms are unlikely to be seen indoors. In spite of the lack of flowers, these are highly ornamental foliage plants, the glossy, dark green leaves looking fresh at all times of the year. *S.arboricola* (syn. *Heptapleurum arboricolum,* Green rays) came to us from South-East Asia where it is wild, principally in Taiwan. This is a splendid evergreen for indoors with a neat manner of growth and a fairly narrow outline. The upright, willowy stems support many compound leaves, collectively rounded in outline. These have a dull surface and are dark olive-green in colour. Plant these in tubs or large pots for use where a bold evergreen effect is required.

Cultivation Grow these eventually large, favourite decorator plants in the shade with a minimum temperature of 10°C (50°F). Water the pots well during the plant's active growing period. Attention to humidity requirement during hot weather is important; a daily light misting over with rain water will be appreciated at this time. When dormant, or in times of particularly dull cool weather, the plants need to be kept dry and warm (this applies to both compost as well as foliage). At such times allow the pots to become almost dry between each good soak. Young specimens can receive a monthly feed with dilute liquid fertiliser. Older plants prefer either a side-dressing of dry fertiliser, which should be well watered in, or a little composted organic manure mixed with potting soil and used as an annual mulch. Pruning may need to be done on occasion. Some stems can be removed altogether by cutting them away during the winter months. This operation needs to be done only when they get too drawn up and top-heavy. Protect all wounds from infection by painting them with a semi-liquid grafting wax preparation. New plants are produced from seed, which is unlikely to be available to the average 'indoor gardener'.

Scindapsus (Araceae)

This is a group of over 20 species of rather fleshy-leaved climbers from South-East Asia. There, in their 'jungle' type habitat, they go through two distinct growth phases; the juvenile leaf form is the one normally encountered in room plants. They display a generally broadly ovate leaf outline. In the wild, *Scindapsus* are tall-growers, climbing by means of their rooting stems. In the home however, they can be kept down to a manageable size without spoiling their natural effect in any way.

Description *S.aureus* (syn. *Rhaphidophora aurea*, Devil's ivy, Golden pothos) is a popular, much-branched climber originally from the Solomon Islands. It has flexible stems, bearing thick, almost succulent, ovate or unequal-sided heart-shaped leaves. These are dark green, heavily streaked and marked with golden-yellow areas. *S.a.* 'Marble Queen' is a cultivar in which, as the name suggests, the leaves are heavily marbled. The colour of these, instead of yellow, as in the original, is creamy-white and the marbling so dense on some of the leaves as to obscure their dark green background. In *S.a.* 'Tricolour', the colour mutation goes a step further, with leaves streaked and spotted in white, yellow and cream with green lines. *S.pictus argyraeus* (Silver vine)* from Java and Borneo develops several, wiry, climbing stems. These are green, covered with soft, satin-textured, dark green leaves, liberally spangled with tiny silver dots. It is a most attractive plant.

These climbers can be used for a variety of purposes, e.g. individually trained up or around a support or as a centre-piece in a mixed planter. In the wild, some individuals become very tall indeed as they scramble their way up through other vegetation to finally emerge in the light. Fortunately the plants we grow indoors can be kept down to a much lower height by twining their stems around the support and by careful pruning away of superfluous shoots. It should be noted that the plants climb by means of their rooting stems. A more natural effect will therefore be obtained when these are encouraged up a mossed support or perhaps a tree fern stake rather than a cane or rope.

Cultivation Given the conditions that they enjoy, i.e. a semi-shaded, warm, draught-free position, these rewarding plants are easy to grow; the minimum temperature is 13°C (55.5°F). Average amounts of water can be given when high temperature produces extension of growth. Overhead misting can be applied at the same time. At other times the compost only needs watering when it feels dry. The plants can be potted up in either a standard loam-less mixture or a sandy loam compost with peat added. Stock increase is by inserting tip cuttings in moist sand. Rudimentary roots are always present at the leaf nodes which makes propagation that much easier. Place the cuttings in a warm humid place for the roots to develop. Little overhead watering should be given until the roots have formed.

Senecio (Compositae)

This genus, with its world-wide distribution of over 1,500 species, is also possibly the largest group within what is a very large family. In such an extensive collection of species it is not surprising to find that there is considerable variation in the appearance of individuals. In this case they range from small succulent plants to woody perennials, sub-shrubs and even small trees. Their name comes from *senex* (=an old man) because of the white or grey hair-like pappus (or down) on the seeds. Several of the smaller growers — particularly those with succulent stems or leaves, succeed on a sunny window-sill.

Description *S.macroglossus* (Wax or Cape ivy) is an evergreen climber with fleshy, smooth, very dark green, shallowly lobed leaves. The lobes of the leaf appear as triangular points — remarkably ivy-like. The heads of yellow 'daisies' which develop from the upper leaf axils during the summer could prove a shock for someone thinking that they were in fact in the process of cultivating an ivy! This slender-grower, together with *S.m.* 'Variegatus'* with cream leaf-tip variegation, can grow to several times its original height in a single season. Two ways in which to cope with this amount of growth are either to train the smooth stems up some kind of support or to keep nipping the shoot ends back in order to promote a bushy specimen. Yet another use for these is as ground cover in a mixed group but the difficulty with this is the removal of any dead leaves. *S.mikanoides* (German ivy) is at first glance a very similar plant. This also has ivy-shaped leaves, soft and fleshy. The whole plant is smooth to the touch. Once again this may be trained as a bush or climber and makes a pretty plant in a hanger. *S.rowleyanus* (String of beads) has a particularly appropriate common name for the leaves of this unusual plant are completely spherical — in appearance just like clouded glass beads. These are strung on thin pendant stems. In the illustration (p. 159) a young specimen shares a pot with Burro's tail (*Sedum morganianum*).

Cultivation The *Senecio* mentioned above require light shade and a minimum temperature of 8°C (46.5°F). Maintain their compost in a 'just moist' condition — never really wet. Indeed this may be allowed to dry through at times without any damage being apparent on these fleshy leaved plants. Feeding with half-strength liquid fertiliser need only be done rarely; two or three times a year should suffice. Use sandy peat for potting, loam-less potting mix will also be perfectly satisfactory for good growth. Both Wax ivy and String of beads will grow from tip cuttings taken off with just a few leaves. After insertion in damp sand, put them into a shady, warm spot for roots to form. We find that the ivy-like species are very prone to attack from aphid. This is due to the very tender new growth. Fortunately these attacks are easily cleared up with a spray-over on several occasions.

Sedum (Crassulaceae) Stonecrop

This large genus of over 500 species has representatives in every continent except Australasia. The name is derived from the latin *sedo* (=to sit) because of the manner in which some species grow on rocks and walls. These are all succulent herbs or sub-shrubs with either flat or cylindrical, fleshy, bloom- or wax-covered leaves and small four to five-petalled flowers in clusters. *Sedum* are useful for arranging on sunlit shelves or window-sills.

Description *S.adolphi* (Golden sedum, Butter plant) is a Mexican species with short, fat, greenish-yellow leaves (more yellow in winter) on sprawling stems. The leaves on the erect flowering stems are smaller. Starry white flowers are carried in clusters. *S.* 'Golden Glow' is a pretty hybrid bearing larger leaves with a golden-bronze sheen. *S.morganianum* (Burro's tail)* is another half-hardy Mexican developing extremely long prostrate branches which become pendant when grown in hanging baskets. The branches are thickly clustered with fleshy, bloom-covered, overlapping leaves. Small clusters of tiny reddish flowers appear at the extremities of the shoots and are best when placed in light shade. *S.multiceps* is a many-branched, eventualy twiggy, dwarf plant, As the leaves fall progressively from the lower part of the stems, the remaining terminal clusters of green foliage give the plant the appearance of a tiny tree. The clusters of yellow flowers develop during the summer months. *S.palmeri* is another Mexican species which, like the Japanese *S.sieboldii*, we have grown out of doors in Britain. Initially this plant has weak rooting stems which turn to grow upright. The flattened, spathulate (spoon-shaped) glaucous grey leaves make an attractive foil for the hanging clusters of individually rather large flowers. *S.rubrotinctum* (Christmas cheer) is a mat-forming species with small, thickly clustered, fat green leaves which flush bronze-red in well lit situations. It has clusters of yellow blooms. *S.sieboldii* is a useful perennial plant, its red wiry stems clad with stalkless, almost circular, red-margined, grey leaves and producing its flat clusters of bright rose flowers during late autumn. *S.s.* 'Medio-variegatum' has a cream-coloured blotch in the centre of each leaf.

Cultivation Grow the majority in full sun, minimum temperature 7°C (44.5°F). Water the pots sparingly at all times, i.e. only when the compost feels dry; then give them a good soak. As their thick succulent leaves have a capacity for water-holding, under-watering is seldom a problem. Feed only occasionally. Monthly applications with a suitably diluted preparation will suffice. For compost, select an open loamy-type medium with added peat and enough sand to promote sharp drainage. Propagation of the group is simplicity itself. Division of most cuttings of stems, or even single leaves, often strike root and will soon form useful little plants if put directly into their final pots.

Sinningia (Gesneriaceae)

This genus of Brazilian plants, mostly tuberous-rooted, with velvet textured leaves and showy tubular flowers was named in honour of Wilhelm Sinning (1794–1874), head gardener at Bonn University. They require constant warmth and shady conditions.

Description The familar Gloxinia, *S.speciosa,* has opposite, often large, long-stalked, softly hairy leaves, produced in almost stemless clusters. The drooping, bell-shaped flowers of the wild species have now been superseded by larger blooms held erect in shades of pink, violet, red, white, bicoloured, speckled with contrasting colour or double flowered*.

Cultivation Many plants are purchased in flower or bud, enjoyed for several weeks, then discarded when the leaves begin to turn yellow. Gloxinias are perennial and so, with care, after this time may be allowed to dry off gradually. Keep these tubers until the following spring, then shake them from the pot, and re-pot in fresh compost. Dormant tubers may be bought. Pot by twisting them into the surface of a light compost, e.g. leaf mould and sand. Water from the base by plunging the pots to half-depth in a bucket of naturally warm water. Then stand them in a semi-shaded spot indoors for the plants to commence growth. Keep their compost nicely moist during the growth period. Feed at weekly intervals with an organic-based fertiliser. Hot dry air and sunshine encourage red spider mite.

Sonerila (Melastomataceae)

This is a large tropical genus of low-growing herbaceous plants. The attractive flowers are of fleeting duration and *Sonerila* are usually grown for their beautiful leaves.

Description A typical plant of this genus suitable for indoors, *S.margaritacea**, forms a bushy, upright specimen. Its branching stems are red, rather hairy, and carry pairs of unequal-sized, pointed ovate leaves. The leaves are dark green above with depressed veins and a slightly puckered surface. Many pearly grey spots, often merging in the older leaves, cover the upper surface between the veins. Below, the leaves are wine-red in colour. Flowers are produced from the apex of the shoots in corymbs or open clusters. They are small, three-petalled, bright rose in colour.

Cultivation Choose a lightly shaded position with year round warmth, minimum temperature 13°C (55.5°F). They appreciate plenty of water when growing well and moist air at all times. Feed at 2-weekly intervals from spring to autumn. An open compost of equal parts peat, leaf mould and sand (plus a little organic fertiliser) suits them well. Selected clones of *Sonerila* are increased from cuttings to ensure that the stock remains true to type. They root readily when taken as half-matured shoots and inserted into pots of moist sandy peat.

Spathyphyllum (Araceae)

This is a genus of 25 or more species, mainly from the warm areas of Central and South America, but with a single representative in the East Indies. The genus derives its name from the Greek *spathe* (=a broad blade) and *phyllon* (=a leaf), because of the leaf-like shape of the typical spathe (the sheath-like covering of the spadix or inflorescence).

Description These plants, of tropical appearance, have long, oval, mostly pointed, glossy leaves and, at first, a white, arum-like inflorescence which matures to green. Most kinds of *Spathyphyllum* are more suited to hot-house cultivation. Two, however, are useful selections for the home. *S.* 'Mauna Loa' is a hybrid seedling, from the Columbian *S. floribundum,* raised in the USA. It is a low-growing plant developing many crowns of dark green leaves. It is particularly free-flowering over several months, the pure whiteness of the flowers forming a marked contrast to their glossy background. *S. wallisii* * is another dwarf, almost stemless, plant which forms a spreading clump. Originally from Columbia and Venezuela, it has thin, oblong (that is to say parallel-sided) bright green leaves with waved edges, each narrowed to a point. The spadix is upright and shorter than its protective white spathe.

These plants are valued for indoor gardens or as individual specimens.

Cultivation *Spathyphyllum* require constant warmth with humidity, minimum temperature 12°C (53.5°F). They should be sited in light shade in order to thrive. In places with a natural high humidity during the summer months, like other plants of tropical origin, they flourish without much trouble. In dry heat they suffer unless misted over with water frequently; in colder places they will require constant heat, once again with misting-over of the leaves. The pots should never dry out but should be kept slightly damp at all times; more water can be given when the plants are growing strongly. Feeding with half-strength liquid fertiliser at 2-weekly intervals is beneficial. Use a compost of equal parts of leaf mould and moist peat plus a little sandy loam, together with some broken charcoal when re-potting. Division of the crowns after the main flowering is over will provide new stock.

Streptocarpus (Gesneriaceae) Cape primrose

This is a genus of over 100 species found naturally in Africa and South-East Asia. The popular indoor plants are hybrids of somewhat involved parentage and are consequently of variable appearance. They are normally grouped under the name *S.* × *hybridus* although they may be seen with the label *S.* × *rexii,* which was one of the principal contributors to the modern plants. Their generic name comes from the Greek words *streptos* (=twisted) and *carpos* (=fruit), which refer to the twisted shape of the seed pods.

Description These are low-growing perennial plants with narrow, oblong, furrowed leaves, frequently of varying sizes, arranged in a stemless often prostrate rosette. The slender unbranched flower stems are erect, bearing from one to several tubular or trumpet-shaped flowers which open wide at the mouth. Both plants as well as flowers vary considerably in size. Some seed-raised strains are robust growers covered in flowers; others, such as *S.* 'Constant Nymph'*, a splendid Dutch-raised cultivar with blue flowers, are of dainty graceful appearance. This and its albino counterpart, *S.* 'White Nymph', are superb indoor plants, easily grown and virtually ever-blooming.

Cultivation These are shade-lovers, requiring high humidity in hot weather and a minimum temperature of 10°C (50°F). Water the pots from below by placing them in a bucket containing tepid water. Avoid getting the leaves wet when ever this is possible. Less water may be given in winter but do not let the compost become dry at this time. A period of semi-dormancy can be induced by keeping the plants cool with less water. A burst of renewed energy will follow this rest. A rich soil is suggested for growing really fine specimens. This can be either acid loam-less compost or, if made up at home, should comprise 1 part of well rotted manure to 2 parts peat and 1 part loam with enough sand added to facilitate sharp drainage. New plants can be raised from seed. This is particularly fine, requiring extreme care when sowing on the surface of well drained compost. Perhaps easier for the amateur is the division of the crowns although not all will divide in this way. Nurserymen increase the named plants from leaf cuttings. After removing a strong healthy leaf, nick the main and secondary veins in a few places before placing the leaf, top-side uppermost, on damp sand in a propagator.

Syngonium (Araceae) Goose foot

Climbing or trailing plants with attractive foliage, originally from tropical Central and South America, make up this genus of nearly 20 species. The botanical name comes from *syn* (=joined) and *gone* (=womb), and derives from the fact that the ovaries are united. Most species bear either arrow- or heart-shaped juvenile leaves which are the ones normally seen under indoor conditions. Later stages of growth have the adult leaves changed in form, becoming divided into several leaflets. The flowers, or rather the inflorescence, comprises a boat-shaped spathe and the typical club-like spadix of the family in which the male and female flowers are separate.

Description *S.hoffmanii* (Goose foot) are creeping or trailing plants and, when young, have the familiar arrow-shaped leaves of the genus. In this species they are greyish with silver centre and veins. *S.podophyllum* (African evergreen) has many attractive forms and cultivars which have been developed from the wild tropical Mexican original. One frequently used to decorate our homes, which is sometimes sold as *Nephthytis triphylla*, but is more correctly called *Syngonium podophyllum* 'Lineatum' or 'Albo-lineatum*', has young leaves which are pointed, heart-shaped, dark glossy green in colour with the central portion and veins distinctly silver. *S.p.* 'Atro-virens' has hastate, or waisted, leaves in which the dark green is heavily shaded with greyish-white. *S.p.* 'Green Gold' (*S.podophyllum* × *xanthophilum*) is a splendid selection with distinctly arrow-shaped leaves, heavily suffused and variegated with yellow-green. *S.wendlandii*, which originally came from Costa Rica, has its deep green three-lobed leaves veined in silver. A plant of dainty appearance, much valued when young, it later develops leaves which lose the silver coloration.

When first purchased, the young plants consist of a cluster of often robust leaves but before very long their trailing stems appear. Although to a certain extent these may be pruned back we find that the leaves are displayed best when the stems are allowed to climb a trellis or even a room divider. Smaller plants can be housed in a dish garden or planter where their bold leaves will be displayed to advantage.

Cultivation A position in light shade should be found for this group. Warm conditions are essential with even a winter night temperature of at least 12°C (55.5°F) being needed. Indeed a sustained temperature of 10°C (50°F) or lower will not be tolerated for long. The plants may be watered freely at all times. Any light humus-rich soil will suit them. They will also grow in plain water with added nutrient. Grown normally, the young plants should not need feeding with additional liquid fertiliser more than say three or four times per season. Stem cuttings of these climbing shrubs will root if each is taken complete with a leaf or two. Place these in a propagator with bottom heat provided.

Tradescantia (Commelinaceae) Spiderwort

The spiderworts are a genus of herbaceous plants from America, more often than not having glassy, succulent stems. *Tradescantia* commemorates John Tradescant (d. 1638) the famous gardener to Charles I of England. Their common name is said to stem from the use, by early settlers in America, of the juice of *T.virginiana* against venomous spiders.

Description Species which are suitable for the greenhouse or indoors are generally short-lived trailing plants with attractive foliage. Additionally the three-petalled flowers, although small, may be carried profusely, thus increasing the plants' interest. *T.albiflora* (Inch plant, Wandering Jew) is a trailer with shiny green, ovate leaves. *T.a.* 'Albo-vittata'*, a sport or mutation, has larger leaves with alternate dark green and white stripes similar to the cultivar 'Silver Queen'. *T.a.* 'Tricolor' has pale green leaves streaked with white.

T.blossfeldiana is a strong grower with downy, curving, erect stems clad with purple-backed, dark green leaves. The clusters of white-centred pink flowers are liberally displayed in the summer. *T.fluminensis* 'Variegata' (Wandering Jew) is a popular indoor plant with its weak stems rooting wherever they come into contact with the soil. The leaves are pointed ovate, striped with green and white. These plants find a ready use in hangers or baskets, their leafy stems developing in a most attractive way.

Cultivation These are adaptable, particularly easy plants in sun or light shade with a minimum temperature of 10°C (50°F). Water them freely from the time that the plants are well established in their pots, rather less until then or in dull weather. Do not allow their leaves to remain wet overnight during cold days in winter. Light feeding will be required if loam-less compost is used. One application per month when the plants are developing should prove sufficient. These plants thrive in virtually any compost. A mixture of peat, leaf mould and sand is frequently used for them. Most of these species tend to spoil eventually, becoming straggly after two or three seasons. Propagating new plants is often a better course than cutting back old ones. Fortunately these are very easy to increase from cuttings. Simply detach the shoots by breaking or cutting them at a swollen leaf node on the stem and inserting three to five of them into a pot of prepared compost. Place the filled pots in a diffused light position for 3 weeks after which time the roots should be forming. Pinching out the tips promotes bushiness. Little is gained in transplanting the rooted cuttings if normal potting compost is used for rooting them. Cuttings will be found to root just as easily if they are put into a jar of plain water.

Vanda (Orchidaceae)

The great family of orchids containing as it does over 15,000 species which are, in turn, allocated to over 600 genera, is virtually worldwide in its distribution. Although we tend to think of them as solely tropical plants, a great many, particularly the smaller terrestrial sorts, occur in temperate to cooler parts of the world. As cultivated plants, orchids hold a great interest with a considerable following in almost every country. These plants, both the more interesting ones and the spectacular species and hybrids, now said to number over 30,000 are normally accommodated in glass-houses (or lath-houses in the tropics). There are some kinds suitable for growing indoors inside a window or elsewhere. The genus *Vanda* just comes into this group. Although perhaps not the best choice of orchid for growing in a room, the species described has, and indeed is, being grown in such a situation. *Vanda* is a genus of epiphytic or air plants which grow naturally among the lower branches of trees. There are some 50 species in the genus and among its members are so many beautiful plants that some people consider this to be the most stately genus in the whole order. The name, Hindu in origin, records the fact that the original introductions came from India, that country being the headquarters for the group, with others coming from Malaysia and the East Indies.

Use these orchids either as temporary display — the blooms can last for 2 months or longer, or in a window-garden. This is a specially adapted window, of good depth with ample light, which retains a high relative humidity because of a further glass partition between the plants and the room.

Description *V.tricolor suavis* (syn. *V.suavis*, Cowslip-scented orchid)* is an upright-growing epiphyte with woody stems clad with two ranks (or rows) of bright green, strap-shaped leaves. The many-flowered lateral racemes of blooms appear from the upper leaf axils during the late winter and spring. Individually these have spathulate (spoon-shaped) petals and sepals, at first flat then twisted. The back of the wax-like, scented flowers is plain white with the upper surface white smothered in rose-magenta spots. The plants are ornamental even when out of flower.

Cultivation *Vanda* need bright light for flower bud initiation. This should be diffused in very hot weather. The minimum temperature is 15°C (59°F). High temperature is particularly necessary during their main period of growth — say spring and early summer. This must be accompanied by equally high humidity brought about by regular syringing. Ample water should also be available to the plants at this time. During partial dormancy, less water is needed as well as lower temperatures. The compost must always remain moist. The use of clay pots with clear drainage is suggested. Although the plants may be staked they will eventually become leggy or too tall. Cut the stems just below active roots. (This will be in spring when new green points appear on the aerial roots.) Swirl the roots around in a pot half-filled with orchid compost, then fill to the correct depth. Compress this and water well to help it settle. After about a year, the plants may be fed at 2-weekly intervals with diluted water-soluble fish fertiliser. Do not destroy the old plants, for new buds break to form fresh stems.

Vriesea (Bromeliaceae)

This large genus of valuable indoor plants from Central and South America belongs to the great family of bromeliads which numbers over 1,800 species. The name *Vriesea* commemorates Dr W. H. de Vriese (1802–62), Professor of Botany at Leyden University, Holland. They are perennial herbaceous plants and, like many other bromeliads, form symmetrical rosettes of, in this case, stiff, unarmed, leathery evergreen leaves, frequently enblazoned with bold zebra-like striping, as well as other attractive patterning. The red or yellow flowers are carried in large spikes, each individually held in a colourful, long-lasting bract. In the wild, *Vriesea* are epiphytes growing on rocks or on the stems and branches of forest trees. Their leaf bases overlap to form an effective water-holding cup — a very useful provision to tide the wild plants over a drought. In cultivation, this facility also has its use, allowing what would normally be a difficult tropical subject to be grown in an unnatural dry air environment indoors. However, these are not the easiest of the group to grow indoors, due to their high temperature/humidity requirement, but they will settle down if extra care is taken during the first few weeks of acclimatisation.

Description *V.pulmonata** has clustered light green rosettes from which emerge branched stems of deep red bracts hiding the yellow flowers. *V.splendens* (Flaming sword) from Guyana forms a sturdy rosette of blunt-ended dark green leaves. These are cross-banded with dark purple stripes. Their short-lived, yellow tubular flowers are carried on a tall upright spike of highly decorative overlapping red bracts which last well in colour for many weeks. Use these plants as flowering specimens for a bold eye-catching display or as attractive foliage plants in a mixed container.

Cultivation This group has to be placed in the shade with a minimum temperature of 15°C (59°F). As noted, high humidity is required at all times, which means a misting-over with a fine atomiser spray daily, preferably more frequently in hot weather. The water-retaining cup must be kept topped up with rain water and the compost damp but not water-logged. Feeding the plants with an organic or water-soluble chemical fertiliser may be carried out monthly. Dilute this to half the suggested strength and apply this to both the reservoir and the compost. Plants may be grown in a very open mixture of peat, kibbled fir bark, and leaf mould. As epiphytes or air plants, the roots are largely needed to anchor the crown of leaves and it is essential for the growing medium to be free-draining. Propagation is from the replacement offshoots produced. Some plants seem reluctant to develop more than one of these at a time. Other care consists of keeping the leaves clean by gently wiping them with a soft cloth moistened in just warm water to which a single drop of liquid detergent has been added. If, due to dry air conditions, the leaf tips brown off these should be carefully trimmed back to living tissue, mimicking the original shape as you do so.

Note: If rain water is unobtainable for diluting the liquid fertiliser try adding the merest drop of household vinegar to normal tap water. The very slight acidulation is both beneficial to the plant and assists in freeing the soluble salts in the feeding material.

Zebrina (Commelinaceae)

This American genus comprises four species of trailing plant. Their name is a Latinized form of the Portuguese word *zebra* and refers to the noticeable longitudinal stripes on the upper leaf surface of *Z.pendula.* This species, like *Tradescantia,* to which it is closely related, makes a fine specimen for hanging baskets.

Description *Z.pendula* (Wandering Jew)* is easy to grow, with fleshy stems, often self-rooting at the nodes. The leaves are oval-pointed, green with glistening silver stripes and stained bright purple underneath. The flowers, in two leafy bracts, are also purple.

Cultivation For preference select a light position away from the full glare of the sun, minimum temperature 7°C (44.5°F). Free amounts of water are needed during the plants' maximum period of growth. Amounts at other times should be regulated strictly according to need. Once the pots are full of roots, feed with dilute liquid fertiliser at 2-weekly intervals throughout the growing season. This is especially important when the plants are grown in the recommended soil-less compost. Insert tip cuttings at almost any time of the year. Snippets placed in a tumbler of water will begin to produce strong white roots within a week or so. After potting them up, pinch out the growing tips in order to develop a bushy plant. Incidentally as many as three cuttings can go into a single pot.

Index of Common Names

Numbers in **bold** refer to colour illustrations.

Index of Latin Names